THE VICTORIA HISTORY OF HAMPSHIRE

DUMMER AND KEMPSHOTT, TWO CHALKLAND PARISHES

Jennie Butler and Sue Lane
with contributions from John Hare

VICTORIA
COUNTY
HISTORY

First published 2022

A Victoria County History publication

© The University of London, 2022

ISBN 978-1-915249-08-1

Typeset in Minion pro
Published by the University of London Press
Senate House, Malet Street, London WC1E 7HU
https://london.ac.uk/press

CONTENTS

LIST OF ILLUSTRATIONS

All photographs are by Jennie Butler or John Hare unless otherwise stated. All maps are drawn by Cath D'Alton and © University of London unless otherwise stated.

Figures

Maps

FOREWORD

THE IDEA OF A NATIONAL series of town and parish histories for every county in England was first mooted at Queen Victoria's Diamond Jubilee in 1897 and the Victoria County History (VCH) was dedicated to her. In 2012, Her Late Majesty Queen Elizabeth II agreed to the rededication of the project to mark her own Diamond Jubilee.

Hampshire was the first county to publish a history of each of its parishes in red book volumes (1912) but these contained only leading families, the Church of England and local charities. In 2008 Hampshire also became the first county to undertake a complete revision of a parish in the modern VCH style which includes the social, economic and religious history of the ordinary people. It seems fitting that this volume, the fifth in the new series to be completed in Hampshire, should be published in the year of HM Elizabeth II's Platinum Jubilee. It follows *Mapledurwell* (2012), *Steventon* (2016), *Basingstoke, a Medieval Town, c.1000–c.1600* (2017) and *Cliddesden, Hatch and Farleigh Wallop* (2018).

Dummer and Kempshott, Two Chalkland Parishes by Jennie Butler and Sue Lane, with contributions from John Hare, provides a fascinating picture of life through the centuries in small farming communities, a life that was often hard – working thin chalk soil with oxen and horses – but also one in which co-operation and mutual support played an essential role. Whilst Kempshott has been swallowed up by an ever-expanding Basingstoke, Dummer retains, at least visually, many of the characteristics of its earlier rural existence. It is amongst Hampshire's most beautiful villages, although transformed from an agricultural to a largely commuter population.

The project is undertaken entirely by volunteer historians, its costs met by book sales, donations and grants. Help and support is needed to enable the work which remains to be done to complete the parishes in the Basingstoke area and, ultimately, the rest of the historic county of Hampshire. I am sure this volume will not only interest people living locally, now and in the future, but also a much wider audience beyond Hampshire and I commend this readable and scholarly parish history to you.

Nigel Atkinson
HM Lord Lieutenant of Hampshire

ACKNOWLEDGEMENTS

THE PARISH HISTORIES of Dummer and Kempshott add to the growing number of others in the Basingstoke district published as part of the new Victoria County History (VCH) of Hampshire. The main authors are Jennie Butler and Sue Lane, with the chapter on landownership written by John Hare, with a contribution from Daniel Spencer. Other members of the VCH Hampshire team contributed their particular expertise and a special debt is owed to Mary Oliver for her paragraphs on early settlement and to Bill Fergie and Edward Roberts for the section on later settlement and buildings. The resources of Hampshire Record Office including a series of manorial court records, the diaries of lord of the manor, Stephen Terry, and the enclosure map of 1743 (reproduced on the book cover) provided particularly rich material, whilst the HRO staff gave unfailingly helpful support.

Julian Jones, chair of Dummer parish council, Barry Dodd, Andrew Ferguson, Sheila Harden, Lyn Hardy, David Miller, Stafford Napier and Charles Palmer-Tomkinson provided local information. They were all generous with their time and knowledge, as were many other parishioners. Sadly, it did not prove possible to trace Christopher Golding, whose unpublished dissertation on Kempshott Park was a valuable asset.

Permission to reproduce illustrations is gratefully acknowledged from the following bodies and individuals: Hampshire Record Office, the Museum of English Rural Life at the University of Reading, the National Portrait Gallery, Historic England Archive, Matthew Beckett at Lost Heritage, Oxford Dictionary of National Biography, Lord Portsmouth, Stafford Napier, John Chapman and Sylvia Seeliger. Attempts to contact Alistair Fitzroy proved unsuccessful. We are also grateful to the Victoria County History Trust for their grant to finance the drawing of the excellent maps for this volume.

Finally, our thanks go to the VCH central office team and the General Editor Adam Chapman as well as to Emma Gallon, Book Manager, University of London Press, for seeing *Dummer and Kempshott, Two Chalkland Parishes* through to its finished form.

INTRODUCTION

DUMMER IS A SMALL, RURAL chalkland parish whose manors are mentioned in Domesday Book and which has a rich history for its modest size. The name *Dummer,* indicating a mere or lake on or by a dun or hill, has had variant spellings including *Dummere, Dunmere, Dommere, Dompmere* and *Dummur.*[1] While no evidence of a lake has been found, the hilly countryside has delighted many, including the curate, James Hervey, who wrote in May 1737 thus:

> The lovely landscape ... a lane set on either side with lofty trees and humble shrubs ... the wheat in blade and sprung up in goodly array ... the folds full of sheep and lambs ... [the country] overlain with a profusion of flowers, the warbling of the nightingale on entering a wood.[2]

Sheep and corn were indeed the basis of the economy, as was the case in the chalkland parishes of the north Hampshire downs. From the mid 16th century the parish is very well documented. Manorial court records, coupled with probate material, provide a detailed picture of farming in the open fields and commons, a system which continued until enclosure transformed the parish in 1743.

Dummer was distinguished by an unusual level of Protestant nonconformity in the late 17th century, followed by the strongly evangelical outlook in the following century when John Wesley, co-founder of Methodism, visited and preached in All Saints' church. The diaries of Stephen Terry (1774–1867), lord of the manor and a staunch upholder of the established church, offer a fascinating insight into the interests of a country squire. They include his passion for hunting and a social life involving the future King George IV, Jane Austen and the leading families of north Hampshire; the farm workers involved in the Swing Riots of 1830; the founding of a Primitive Methodist chapel; the formation of two Friendly Societies and a visit by Joseph Arch, president of the National Agricultural Labourers' Union. The diaries present a contrasting picture of life for many parishioners. The sale of the estate in 1926 ended centuries of traditional lordship.

Kempshott, the house, park and two farms, was added to the parish in 1879. Thereafter, the parish was known as *Dummer with Kempshott,* and its history for just over 100 years until the transfer of Kempshott to Basingstoke in 1985, forms part of this volume.[3] Kempshott's earlier history was entwined with Dummer from the later Middle

---

1   *Domesday*, 121 (and index, 1339); TNA, CP 25/1/203/1/8; *Feudal Aids* II, 313; TNA, SC 2/212/14; HRO, 93M96/3/1; Ekwall, *English Place-Names*, 146.

2   J. Hervey, *A collection of the letters of the late Reverend James Hervey – to which is attached an account of his life and death* (London, 1763), 31–8.

3   The Kempshott described in this book has either been absorbed into Basingstoke or remains part of Dummer parish. The area of west Basingstoke known as Kempshott since 1908 is not connected; its

Ages. It became a detached part of Winslade parish from 1393 but by the 19th century, its small population became related to Dummer for all practical purposes. Variations on the name have included *Campessete*, *Kempeschete* and *Kembeshute*; the first element of the name 'kemp' (OE *cenep*) suggests a plant name, while 'shott' (OE *scēat*) refers to land.[4] Kempshott with two 'ts' has been used throughout the book unless part of a direct quotation.

In 2020 Dummer remained a quiet rural village whose historic core was designated as a Conservation Area in 1981. While surrounded by agricultural fields, few in the parish worked on the land, the population consisting largely of commuters and retirees. The ever-expanding development of Basingstoke as the town extended in a south-westerly direction was the cause of very considerable concern. Land north of the M3 London to Southampton motorway (opened in 1971) had either been developed or designated for development, while suburban housing estates altered the nature of the parish and added significantly to the population.

Boundaries and Parish Origins

The parish of Dummer, originally within Bermondspit hundred, lies five miles (8 km) from the centre of Basingstoke but adjacent to its south-western suburbs. It is one of a line of parishes on the slopes of the north Hampshire downs with Mapledurwell, Winslade and Cliddesden to the north-east and Popham to the south. Farleigh Wallop and Nutley lie to the east and North Waltham, Oakley and Deane to the west. The parish measures three miles north to south and two miles west to east with a south-west to north-east axis. It is approximately rectangular with an irregularly shaped part of the parish lying north of the M3 motorway and a small bite taken out in the south near Grange farm. This square shape of the parish, together with neighbouring Farleigh and North Waltham, is found on chalkland plateaux in this part of Hampshire rather than the more common linear shape where parishes run back from a river or up the scarp slope of the downs. The parish has always been entire with no detached parts.

Dummer contained three manors, East and West Dummer and the Grange. The Grange, in the south, had been held by Waverley Abbey (Surr.) from the 12th century until shortly after the dissolution of the monasteries. All three had come into common ownership by 1597.[5] The Grange contained 304 a. of land and was always worked as a single farm, unlike the rest of the parish. Prior to enclosure, agriculture was carried out in common fields and the downlands provided common pasture. An Act of Parliament of 1743 brought about the enclosure of 1,789 a. of land.[6] In 1870 the parish area was 2,180 a.[7]

The boundaries in the west, south and east have changed very little whereas the northern perimeter has seen several extensions and contractions. The original western

---

naming caused confusion at the time and continues to do so.
4   *Domesday*, 107; *Rot. Hund.* II, 221; *Feudal Aids* II, 332; Ekwall, *English Place-Names*, 258.
5   Below, Landownership.
6   HRO, 120M97/1.
7   http://www.visionofbritain.org.uk/place/4697 (accessed 29 Sept. 2019).

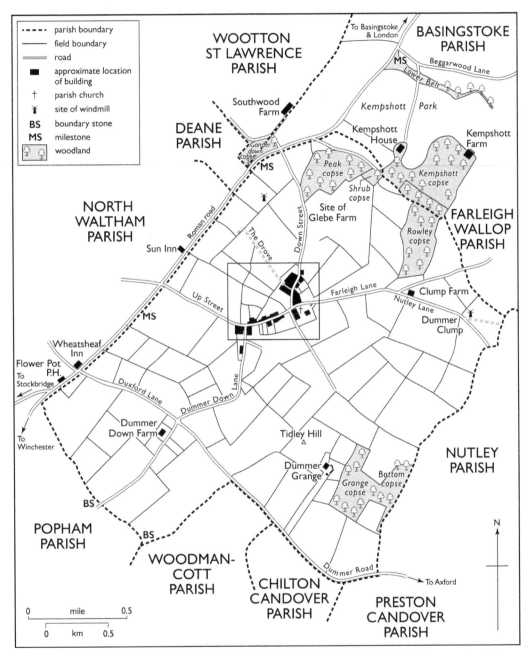

Map 1 *Dummer and Kempshott in the 1870s based on the 1:10,560 OS 1st edn and 1838 tithe map; for village detail inset see Map 2.*

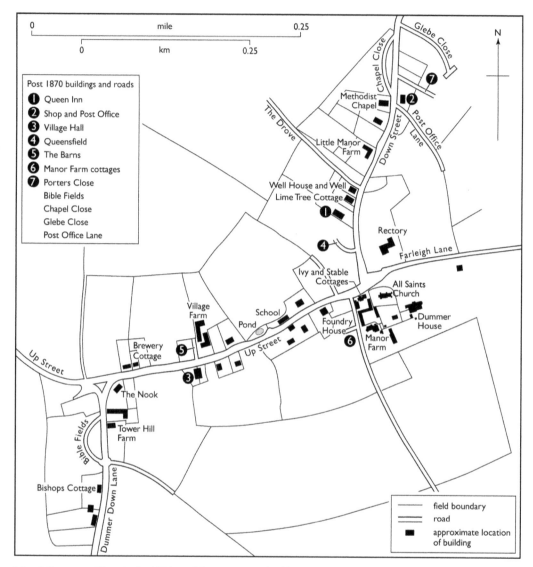

Map 2 *Dummer village in the 1870s with later structural additions.*

edge, which survived in 2020, follows the Silchester to Winchester Roman east–west road and then part of the London to Penzance road (A30). Close to the Wheatsheaf Hotel and Flower Pot Cottages (formerly Flower Pot public house), the Basingstoke to Winchester road (A33) forks and marks the most south-western point of the parish. From there the boundary turns south-east and in 2020 passed under two motorway slip roads and the M3 at the Popham Interchange to follow undulating fields and woodland edges. Two stones define the perimeter at either end of Popham Down Copse. These display the letters D and M, which presumably refer to Dummer and Micheldever. The boundary then continues along the woodland edge before joining and following Dummer Road to Ewedown Copse, the southernmost point of the parish. It then turns north, ascending through farmland and woods to Nutley Lane near Dummer Clump and Inwood Copse

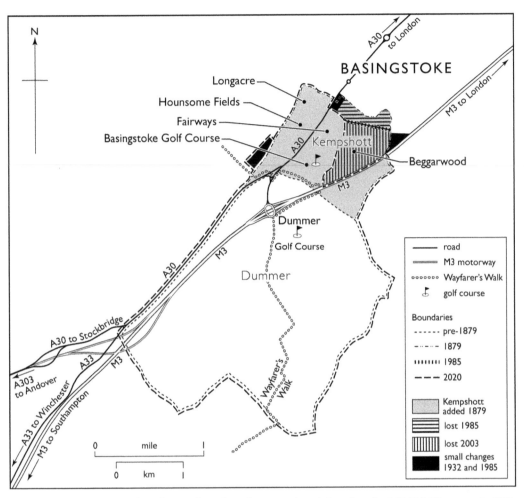

Map 3 *Dummer and Kempshott showing boundary changes and roads based on the 1:25,000 OS map, as in 2020.*

then north-west towards Rowley Copse. Before Kempshott was added to the parish the northern boundary curved past Rowley, Shrub and Peak Copses and then south returning to the turnpike road.

In 1879, following the Divided Parishes Act of 1876, 555 a. of Kempshott, then a detached part of Winslade parish, was united with Dummer, comprising Kempshott House, ancillary buildings, paddocks, garden, parkland and Kempshott Farm (later known as Kennel Farm).[8] The northern boundary was redrawn to run north-east from Rowley Copse between Kempshott and Shortwood Copses, along the western edge of Sullinger Copse and along the sinuous strip of Lower Belt woodland edging the north of Beggarwood Park. It then crossed the turnpike road to the Roman road before turning

8   LGBO 10.105, 8 Dec. 1879; TNA, OS 27/2187; OS map 1:10,560 (1872 edn), sheet 26.5; *P.O. Dir. 1885*, 650; below, Landownership.

Figure 1 *Curve of trees at Popham Down Copse forming the parish boundary.*

south and descending to Southwood farm. To reflect this extension, the parish name was changed to *Dummer with Kempshott* in 1886.[9]

In 1932 a 4 a. plot north of the Basingstoke golf course was transferred to Basingstoke.[10] A boundary reorganisation from 1985 saw the loss of Beggarwood Park to Basingstoke (67 a.) but Dummer gained 15 a. from Farleigh Wallop parish as well as the Southwood farm buildings and 34½ a. from Oakley parish.[11] The parish name formally reverted to *Dummer* in 1989.[12] The Beggarwood housing estate developed from 2001 on 118 a. of land north of the M3 motorway was transferred to Basingstoke in May 2003[13] when the boundary changed again to run down the centre of the M3 motorway, along the eastern edge of Basingstoke golf course and back to the A30. In 2020 Dummer parish was 2,597 a.[14]

9   TNA, OS 27/2187; LGBO 20.332.
10   HRO, 24M95/2; OS map 1:10,560, XVIII.SW.
11   *Basingstoke and Deane (Parishes) Order 1985*, 179; HRO, H/CS6/1/6.
12   *Basingstoke and Deane Dist. Council, Parish Name Change*, 27 July 1989.
13   BDBC Planning app., BDB 40026; *Basingstoke and Deane (Parishes) Order 2003 no. 846.*
14   BDBC, Research & Data sect.

Landscape

The underlying geology is upper chalk with superficial deposits of clay with flint. A narrow strand of surface alluvial deposit lies in a shallow valley curving north of Dummer Down farm along which Dummer Road runs, suggesting a palaeochannel of a lost river rising in the hills to the south beyond the parish.[15] There are no apparent surface water courses within the parish but an underground stream is reported to flow from the Clump beneath Dummer Grange farm and on to the Candovers.[16] At times of heavy rain, a winterbourne rises at Dummer Clump and flows along Farleigh Lane and Down Street, which can cause flooding.[17] A small duck pond lies in Up Street and dew ponds collect at Clump and Dummer Down farms. The lord of the manor, Stephen Terry, excavated a pond in front of Dummer House adjacent to Nutley Lane but by 1896 it had been infilled as part of the gardens.[18] Two small ponds lie in the fields east of Tower Hill farm and man-made water features appear on both Basingstoke and Dummer golf courses.

The landscape gently undulates between 459 ft. (140 m.) and 590 ft. (180 m.) rising to its highest point of 675 ft. (206 m.) at Dummer Clump in the east. Open fields

Figure 2 *Track to Dummer Clump.*

15 http://mapapps.bgs.ac.uk/geologyofbritain/home.html?location=dummer&gobBtn=go (accessed 28 Oct. 2018).
16 Charles Palmer-Tomkinson, pers. comm. 2019. Dummer Grange takes its water supply from a 200 ft. well.
17 Sheila Harden, pers. comm. 2019.
18 HRO, 24M49/4; BL, 004830987; OS map 1:25,000 sheet Hants. XXVII.6 (1872 and 1896).

surrounded the village until enclosure in 1743.[19] Views in the mid 18th century to the mid 19th would have featured two windmills: one recorded in 1744 at Dummer Clump, and a second situated behind Chapel Close in what was still known as Millfield in 2020.[20]

In 2020 the linear settlement lay central to the parish surrounded by farmland with fields divided by mixed deciduous hedges, some showing evidence of formerly coppiced hazel trees.[21] The mixed farming of earlier years – arable, sheep, dairy, pigs and grazing – had given way to almost entirely arable farming. Small areas of grassland were found in private paddocks for equine use.[22]

Six blocks of deciduous woodland survive at Kempshott, Peak, Shrub and Rowley copses in the north and Grange and Bottom copses in the south-east. An 8 a. mixed woodland named Sunset Wood, south-west of Clump farm, was planted c.2016 and another north of Dummer Down farm was planted in the 20th century.[23] Basingstoke golf course (106 a.) and Dummer golf course (165 a.) both lie within the parish to the north on either side of the M3 motorway. In 2020 the remains of 21 chalk pits dug for agricultural use, scattered around the parish, were mostly colonised by trees.

Well-wooded parkland was developed at Kempshott from 1788 on plans believed to have been designed by Humphry Repton, landscape architect, to enhance the grandeur of the new mansion and suit the requirements of the Prince of Wales.[24] In 1927 a large part of this was sold to Basingstoke golf club where the course designer preserved much of the rolling topography and mature trees and even fragments of the original pale boundary.

Communications

Roads

The Roman Silchester to Winchester road forms the western parish boundary. This road was turnpiked by the Basingstoke and Stockbridge Trust established in 1756.[25] The tollgate was sited north of Basingstoke Down but in 1801 the trust ordered it to be moved to Kempshott Hill at the junction with Beggarwood Lane. Milestones were erected denoting the distances from London, Basingstoke, Stockbridge and Winchester;[26] three survive within the parish.[27] The trust was terminated in 1878.[28]

19 HRO, 120M97/1.
20 Mills Archive, KIRS-26289, K. Kirsopp, *Notebook of Hampshire Windmills*; HRO, 3M39/1, Greenwood Map 1826; below, Economic History.
21 *Design Statement.*
22 Ibid.; below, Economic History.
23 https://www.google.com/maps/search/dummer (accessed 28 Oct. 2018).
24 Golding, *Kempshot Manor*, 4; www.kempshottmanor.net (accessed 13 Jan. 2020).
25 *Turnpike Trusts. County reports of the Secretary of State, under the act 3 & 4 Wm. IV. cap. 80. No.4.-Hants.* (Parl. Papers 1852 [1521]), 19.
26 HRO, 76M86/40; HRO, Q26/1.
27 NHLE, nos 1416757, Milestone on A30 at Ganderdown; 1096173, Milestone on A30/A303 at NGR SU 597483; 1096174, Milestone on A30/A303 at NGR SU 575460 (accessed 16 Dec. 2021); Hants. HER 54172, 54173.
28 HRO, Q26/2/1; *Turnpike Trusts* (Parl. Paper 1878 [Cd. 353]), LXVI.683.

In 1929 the A30 was widened from Dummer crossroads to Kempshott Hill.[29] A section of the A30 trunk road constructed in the 1930s enters the north as a dual carriageway, but reduces to a single carriageway at Ganderdown and follows the same route as the Roman road and turnpike along what was formerly known as Popham Lane. The construction of the M3 motorway had a major impact, carving a new route together with the associated slip roads and access to Down Street by a roundabout at junction seven. Duxford Lane passes under the motorway to join the A30 opposite the Wheatsheaf Hotel in North Waltham parish (Map 1). Maps pre-dating the motorway show a lane leading west from Up Street to North Waltham crossing the A30 to Maidenthorn Lane. This was truncated and re-routed to the north to emerge opposite the Sun Inn.[30]

All other roads within the parish are narrow lanes radiating from the church; none has pavements and vehicle traffic is limited to 20 mph in the village centre. Down Street and Up Street (formerly Common Street), lined with houses, form a horseshoe-shaped through route from the M3 junction to the A30 at the Sun Inn.

The 1743 estate map depicts a T-junction at the church but by 1864 maps show a track running from Manor farm south to Grange farm.[31] In 2020 this was a bridleway known locally as 'the concrete road' and part of the long-distance Wayfarer's Walk from Litchfield to Emsworth. Farleigh Lane leads east from the church to Farleigh Wallop. Nutley Lane forks off this at Clump Farm, serving Mulberry House, Clump Barn and cottages, but then becomes a by-way towards Dummer Clump before leaving the parish at Nutley Wood. The sunken Dummer Down Lane runs south from Tower Hill farm to Dummer Grange farm in Dummer Road, which in turn runs from the A30 to Axford. A map of 1871 shows a T-junction with Dummer Down Lane and Axford Road.[32] In 1903 a map depicts this as a crossroads with a road leading to Woodmancott passing in front of Dummer Down farmhouse, which explains its orientation sideways on to Dummer Down Lane. In 2020 this junction had reverted to a T-junction with a diverted bridleway a field away from the house before turning to join the earlier south-west route to Woodmancott.[33]

The names of the culs de sac serving 20th-century residential infill such as Glebe Close, Porter's Close, Post Office Lane, Chapel Close, Queensfield, The Barns and Bible Fields reflect the history of the village. Various footpaths cross the parish. One in particular starting beside the cemetery was used for access to the A30 and Sun Inn but was truncated by the motorway.[34] A permissive track following the ancient drove leads from Well Cottage in Down Street to the open fields.[35] The junction of Dummer Down Lane and Up Street is marked by the Seven Sisters triangle planted with six cherry trees.

In the north of the parish there were two carriage drives approaching Kempshott House through the parkland from the Basingstoke to Winchester road. One skirted the edge of Peak Copse and the other joined Beggarwood Lane, passing through the Coachroad Belt woodland. In 2020 the lane was preserved as a cul-de-sac, *Old Beggarwood Lane*, with the earlier line of the road preserved as a footpath linking it to the A30.

29   *The Times*, 8 Aug. 1929.
30   OS map 1:10560 (1960 edn) SU54NE.
31   BL, 004830987.
32   TNA, OS 27/2187.
33   BL, 004830987; HRO, 26M75/7; OS 1:10,560 map XXVI.NW (1897).
34   Sheila Harden, pers. comm. 2019.
35   https://maps.Hants.gov.uk/rightsofwaydefinitivemap/ (accessed 18 Nov. 2019).

Figure 3 *Down Street at entrance to village; houses bordering road, no footpaths.*

Figure 4 *Up Street with pond; houses set back from tree-lined road.*

Post, Carriers, Buses, Services

In 1851 Fanny Holms was named as a letter carrier.[36] Three years later a post office was opened in Up Street opposite the school by James Allen (d. 1881).[37] He was succeeded by his widow, Hannah (d. 1890).[38] Post deliveries from Basingstoke in 1864 were twice daily.[39] By 1885 the post office had moved to Little Manor Farm where farmer Rowland Davis Drinkwater took on the role of postmaster.[40] The nearest money order and telegraph office was in Basingstoke until 1889 when a money order office opened in Worting,[41] both some considerable distance from the village. In 1895 a facility opened in nearby North Waltham.[42] A succession of postmasters can be traced to 1939,[43] and at an unknown date new premises were opened on the opposite side of the road from Little Manor farmhouse on the corner of Post Office Lane but closed in 2006.[44] From May 2007 the village hall hosted a visiting postmaster from Hook one afternoon a week.[45] This ceased in 2015 and from September 2016 the village was served by a mobile office which visited once each week operating out of Barton Stacey.[46] In 2020 a daily collection was made six days a week from street pillar boxes. The nearest post office was in Basingstoke.

George Barber aged 18 was listed as a carrier in 1861, as was his father John in 1871.[47] Between 1895 and 1907 Henry Baker operated as a fly proprietor.[48] John Chivers ran a freight haulage business in 1939.[49] Arthur Cecil Porter moved to Dummer in 1910 and ran the shop and post office as well as a horse-drawn carrier service. This became the Porter's bus service and traditionally conveyed the cricket team to away matches.[50] In 1939 Oswald Porter took over the business, offering taxis, self-drive cars and regular coaches to Basingstoke market on Wednesdays and Saturdays.[51] Two buses ran to Basingstoke on Wednesdays, Fridays and Saturdays. Travellers requiring a service on the other days or at more convenient times could pre-book a motor coach and request a stop at the Sun Inn on the A30 from Shamrock & Rambler Coaches (of Bournemouth) or Royal Blue Coaches which ran services from Bournemouth to London and Exeter to Windsor respectively.[52] In 1941 and 1942 Venture buses ran four or five buses a day to Basingstoke on Wednesdays, Saturdays and Sundays. After the war Venture ran a daily

---

36   *Census,* 1851.
37   https://sites.google.com/site/ukpostofficesbycounty/home/england (accessed 25 Oct. 2018).
38   *Census,* 1881.
39   BL, 004830987.
40   *Census,* 1891; *P.O. Dir. Hants.* 1885, 651; HRO, 67M83/156.
41   *P.O. Dir. Hants.* 1895, 131; 1899, 140; 1903, 144; 1907, 158.
42   *P.O. Dir. Hants.* 1895, 131.
43   *Census,* 1891–1911; *1939 Register; P.O. Dirs Hants.* 1885–1907.
44   *Basingstoke Gaz.,* 28 Dec. 2006.
45   *Basingstoke Gaz.,* 5 June 2007.
46   https://sites.google.com/site/ukpostofficesbycounty/home/england (accessed 25 Oct. 2018); Parish Council Minutes 19 Sept. 2016.
47   *Census,* 1861; 1871.
48   For example, *P.O. Dir. Hants.* (1899), 140. A fly proprietor was a carrier offering a relatively high-speed carrier service with a two-wheeled cart.
49   *1939 Register.*
50   *Hill and Dale,* parish magazine, Jan. 1968, HRO, 65M72/PZ3.
51   *1939 Register; Hants. and Berks. Gaz. Rail & Bus Guide* (1939).
52   HRO, 51M76/H/2B/1.

service with five buses in each direction as well as a late-night service from Basingstoke on Wednesdays, Fridays and Saturdays after the pubs and the cinemas shut.[53] By 1950 a service ran from the Wheatsheaf, a considerable walk from the village, and twice-daily buses ran on Wednesdays and Saturdays from Dummer Grange farm.[54] In 2020 one bus a day was operated by Stagecoach between Steventon and Basingstoke on Mondays and Fridays, with two on Wednesdays.[55]

Mains electricity was supplied to the village in 1950.[56] A public telephone kiosk was erected in Down Street opposite its junction with Chapel Close as an extension of the post office line.[57] BT (previously British Telecom) discontinued support for the payphone in 2016. Three years later the village adopted the kiosk and converted it to an information point and book exchange.[58] A broadband internet connection was installed c.2003/4.[59]

Population

The Domesday survey recorded 25 heads of households in the two manors of East and West Dummer.[60] Using a multiplier of 4.5 persons per household suggests an estimated population of 112, a number broadly comparable with the neighbouring rural parishes.[61] Just 11 inhabitants were assessed for the lay subsidy in 1327 and 15 in 1333, representing the heads of the wealthier households.[62] There is little evidence of the Black Death having had a major effect on Dummer but the gap in identifiable rectors between 1349 and 1392 may be an indication of this.[63] Kempshott had six households in 1086 – three *villani* (tenants with land) and three cottars – and three taxpayers in 1327 but by 1393 there were no parishioners.[64] At that date it was united with Winslade, a parish on the eastern side of Farleigh Wallop; both manors were held by the Tichborne family.[65]

A muster roll of 1524 included 26 men and two women, while a taxation list of the following year recorded 34 names of whom three were female.[66] Approximately half of the names appear on both lists. The overall population increased with the inclusion of the Grange in 1527. Between 1542 and 1641 there were 575 baptisms and 457 burials. Only in 1557–9 did burials (33) outnumber baptisms.[67] This may be related to the influenza pandemic which spread from Asia across Europe to England from 1556 to 1560.[68]

---

53   *Hants. and Berks. Gaz. Rail & Bus Guide* (1941–2).
54   HRO, 5M70/27.
55   www.stagecoachbus.com/timetables (accessed 24 Sept. 2019).
56   HRO, 5M70/27; HRO, 56M82/B87/1.
57   HRO, 96M96/23/3.
58   http://www.dummerparishcouncil.gov.uk/FullCouncil.aspx. 5 Dec. 2016, 20 Nov. 2017 (accessed 21 Nov. 2018).
59   Julian Jones, pers. comm., 2019.
60   *Domesday*, 108, 121; below, Social History.
61   For example, Cliddesden 25, Popham 37, Herriard 11 (*Domesday* 115, 108).
62   *Hants. Tax List 1327*, 41; TNA, E 179/242/15A, rot. 6.
63   Below, Religious History, Social History.
64   *Domesday*, 107; *Hants. Tax List 1327*, 20; *Reg. Wykeham* II, 441–2.
65   Below, Landownership.
66   TNA, E 36/19, 317–18; TNA, E 179/173/183, rot. 13d.
67   HRO, 65M72/PR1.
68   E.A. Wrigley, R.S. Schofield, *The Population History of England 1541–1871* (Cambridge, 1981), 671.

In 1603, 100 communicants were recorded, presumably the greater part of the population, excluding children.[69] The hearth tax return of 1665 had 36 households, a 44 per cent increase since Domesday.[70] In 1673 there were 48 households with a slight drop to 42 in 1675[71] and with the number of communicants also falling to 88.[72] In 1725, the population was c.162[73] and in 1798, 128 men (80 between the ages of 15 and 60) were assessed for a volunteer local army.[74]

In 1801 there were 52 families living in 52 houses with a population of 286.[75] Numbers climbed steadily to 412 in 1841 and households increased to 81.[76] The population remained fairly static at around 400 for three decades.[77] In 1881 the figure was 390 but incorporated 93 persons in 14 households in Kempshott, comprising the family of Sir Nelson Rycroft and live-in servants at Kempshott House, outdoor staff, the bailiff and five households in Kennel Farm Cottages.[78] This disguised a fall in numbers in Dummer in line with a national trend of rural poor moving to the towns.

During the 20th century the population remained at around 400 until 1985 when part of Kempshott was transferred into Basingstoke, resulting in a fall to c.350.[79] This rose dramatically to 643 in 2001 when the Beggarwood housing estate was under construction and became a ward of Dummer parish.[80] The population continued to grow, as indicated by the 956 residents on the Beggarwood electoral roll in 2003. With 328 on the roll for Dummer village ward in the same year, this gave an unprecedented number of 1,284 adults.[81] With the transfer of Beggarwood to Basingstoke in 2003, the population reduced to 466 by 2011.[82] House building continued: Longacres (310 houses) and The Fairways (97 houses)[83] were completed in 2018, when the electoral register showed 744 people over the age of 18,[84] rising further to 898 in February 2020.[85] Further developments at Hounsome Fields (750 houses), Basingstoke golf course (1,100 houses) and a number of smaller sites were under development in 2022.[86]

69 *Dioc. Pop. Returns*, 490; below, Religious History.
70 *Hearth Tax 1665*, 218; below, Landownership.
71 TNA, E 179/176/569, rot. 9d; TNA, E 179/247/30, rot. 19d.
72 *Compton Census*, 83; below, Religious History.
73 *Parson and Parish*, 45, 64.
74 HRO, Q22/1/2/5/16.
75 *Population Rtns 1801–2*, 333; below, Social History.
76 *Population Rtns 1843*, 316; *Census*, 1841.
77 *Census*, 1851–71.
78 *Census*, 1881.
79 *Conservation Area*; BDBC Council Order OP 27.7.89.
80 LGBO 10.105, 8 Dec. 1879.
81 BDBC, Electoral Services.
82 *The Basingstoke and Deane (Parishes) Order 2003* no. 846; *Census*, 2011.
83 Ibid.; *Parish Newsletter*, Spring 2018.
84 Electoral Roll, 2018.
85 Ibid.; BDBC, Electoral Services.
86 *Basingstoke Golf Course Development Brief Supplementary Planning Document Oct. 2019*; BDBC, Planning App. 15/04503/OUT; 19/0071/OUT.

Settlement and Buildings

Early Settlement

The high chalk downs in this area are heavily covered with a drift deposit of clay with flints.[87] This rich source of large flint nodules, the raw material for tool making, was utilised from the earliest settlers intermittently through the Ice Ages (c.500,000 years ago) through to the end of the Bronze Age (c.800 B.C.). Flint implements, notably hand axes of Palaeolithic date (earlier than 10,000 B.C.), were found through fieldwalking near the Sun Inn and south of the high ground at Dummer Clump.[88] Dummer Clump must have been a particularly rich area for good flint, as it was also used in both the Mesolithic (c.10,000–c.4,000 B.C.) and Neolithic periods (to c.3,300 B.C.) for flint working: large numbers of artefacts have been collected.[89] Mesolithic implements were found on Basingstoke golf course.[90] The Sun Inn area was also a prolific flint-working site in the Neolithic Period, with a variety of tools and implements found.[91] A further scatter of Neolithic flakes was found on the southern edge of the parish.[92] It is likely that the flint-working sites were occupied as settlement sites at least temporarily, but there is no evidence for structures due to later natural erosion and agricultural disturbance.

As elsewhere, most of the evidence for the Bronze Age is funerary, including the distinctive round barrows which can still be seen quite commonly in the area, such as one in the south-west corner of the parish, part of a barrow cemetery and another ploughed out and visible as a crop mark.[93] Other barrows are visible on aerial photographs south of Tower Hill farm and at Dummer Clump.[94] One barrow close to Kempshott House was dug into in 1850 and an urn removed.[95] Much less usual, an urnfield with at least 20 cremations was uncovered near the border with Nutley in 1888, and further work on the site in 1967 recovered a further five urns. They were inverted, and each covered by a cist of clay and flint.[96] A further cremation cemetery was excavated at Beggarwood Lane prior to house building in 2016, where seven collared urns were found and at least nine cremations.[97] Some late Bronze Age material was found at Hounsome Fields and Kennel Farm, which may suggest some settlement preceding the main Iron Age occupation of these sites. The uncovering of such large areas prior to house building has led to a more detailed understanding of the area in the Iron Age and early Roman period, with

---

87   OS Geological Survey of Great Britain, Basingstoke sheet 284.
88   Hants. HER 18785; 20297; 59188; D. Roe, CBA Report 8, *Lower and Middle Palaeolithic*; Proc. HFC&AS, vol. 9 pt 2, 180–1; vol.16 pt 3, 253; http://journal.lithics.org/index.php/lithics/article/viewFile/590/575, Wessex Archaeology, *The Southern Rivers Palaeolithic Project* (accessed 13 Nov. 2019).
89   Hants. HER 20290; 20291.
90   Willis Museum card index for SU 59624740.
91   Hants. HER 18782.
92   Hants. HER 18391.
93   Hants. HER 18436; L.V. Grinsell, 'Hampshire Barrows III', *Proc. Hants. F.C.*, 14.3 (1940), 349–50.
94   Hants. HER 63936; 20337.
95   Hants. HER 18783.
96   Hants. HER 26622; 26624.
97   Hants. HER 69775; R. Kennedy and R. Massey, 'An Early Bronze Age Cremation Cemetery at Beggarwood, Lane, Basingstoke 2016', *Proc. HFC&AS, Hampshire Studies*, 74 (2019).

ditch systems probably extending between these two sites and the 32 a. just north of the Winchester road, indicating an integrated landscape.[98] There were a number of post-built structures within enclosures, storage pits, a small late cremation cemetery and pottery going through to the Roman period, *c.*100 A.D.[99] The area has been surveyed from the air and the photographs of cropmarks indicate more settlements of the same character, with ditches and enclosures.[100] There is further Roman evidence of occupation in the south-east corner of the parish near Breach Cottages,[101] but by far the most significant Roman site lies around the Wheatsheaf Inn. The Roman road between Silchester and Winchester runs in front of the inn and there have been finds since the 19th century indicating that this place was probably of regional importance, midway between the two cantonal capitals. Land clearance in connection with the M3 motorway resulted in rescue excavations which recovered quantities of building materials, pottery both local and imported, jewellery and coins indicating occupation from the 1st to 4th centuries A.D.[102] Coins and other small finds continue to be discovered.[103]

Medieval Settlement and Buildings[104]

Domesday Book records two manors in Dummer with each claiming a church, suggesting that there may originally have been two settlements. One focus, the east manor, can clearly be recognised round the church, the later rectory and the main manor house (Dummer House) and Manor Farm. From this point the topography determined whether one went uphill along Up Street or gently downhill along Down Street. The second focus is less obvious, but may be represented by the small green at the junction of Up Street and Dummer Down Lane. Subsequent infill development between these groupings has strengthened the linear pattern of the settlement while largely maintaining its historic boundaries.

The earliest surviving domestic buildings are timber-framed with wattle and daub infill. The earliest evidence for brick construction dates from the early 17th century in high-class construction as at Dummer Grange, or for limited use as in chimney stacks. By the 18th century brick building had become standard, whether for refacing earlier structures or for new building. The village has many surviving brick farmhouses. At an elite level, brick became less fashionable at the beginning of the 19th century, and both Kempshott House and Dummer House were refaced in stucco. In 2022, traditional buildings possess a variety of roofing material: thatch, tile and slates; most would have been thatched earlier.

---

98   Hants. HER 69775; 63840; 69102.

99   R. Massey and M. Nichol, 'Iron Age and Roman Enclosed Settlement at Winchester Road Basingstoke', *Proc. HFC&AS Hampshire Studies*, 74 (2019).

100 Hants. HER 38264; 63861; 63934; 63937.

101 Hants. HER 18845; 18846.

102 Hants. HER 18747; 18757; D. Charlton, 'The Wheatsheaf, Dummer, Hampshire: an archaeological rescue investigation', *BAHS Newsletter*, 21 (2015), 14–15.

103 Inf. from Mary Oliver.

104 The following section and dating is by Edward Roberts and Bill Fergie and draws on intensive study of the vernacular buildings of the area: see E. Roberts, *Hampshire Houses; Their Dating and Development* (HCC, 2003).

Dummer's medieval church is sited at a right-angle junction of two roads. Standing next to the church is Manor Farm, which probably occupies the site of the medieval manor farm, although surviving fabric is later.[105] Nevertheless, three medieval domestic buildings do survive. The Nook in Up Street, a cruck-framed, open-hall house, has been dated by dendrochronology to 1420–4.[106] Lime Tree Cottage in Down Street, whose precise building date is not known, is also a cruck-framed building. Cruck houses were relatively common in rural Hampshire between about 1300 and 1500 and Dummer is one of only a few villages where more than one has survived.[107] The only other medieval, open-hall house that has been identified is Bishops Cottage, which stands at the southern extremity of the village near Tower Hill farm on Dummer Down Lane. Two of its three early bays may have formed the original house and one of these was clearly the open hall, whose rafters are heavily soot-blackened from the former open fire below. The precise sequence of building or rebuilding might be determined by tree-ring dating but no such exercise has been undertaken. The form of the house and its timber-framing suggest a building date of around 1500. These three medieval houses in Down Street, Up Street and as far as Dummer Down Lane indicate the possible extent of the medieval village.

Post-Medieval Settlement and Buildings

Bricks were infrequently used in this part of Hampshire in 1500, and yet a century later they were commonly in use, even in timber-framed houses. Well House, Down Street, a timber-framed, lobby-entry house of c.1600, was built with a brick chimney to heat the hall and probably for cooking too. The chimney contained the smoke from the hall fire so that a first-floor chamber could be built above. This chamber also had its own brick fireplace. There are indications at the north-western end of the house that the framing may incorporate elements of an earlier house, but it has not been the subject of a dating exercise.[108] Well House is presumably named because it adjoins one of the village wells. This one is particularly deep (248 ft., 86.6 m.) and has a well house over it which contains a manually driven winding wheel. This well house was built in traditional timber-framed form in 1879.[109]

The earliest part of Manor Farm House, also dating to c.1600, has timber-framed walls but, as a superior feature, some of the timber panels are infilled with bricks carefully laid in a herringbone pattern. At an even more superior level, Dummer Grange, the finest 17th-century house in the parish, has walls made entirely from brick.[110]

Later Development

There was already considerable variation in house sizes, reflected in the hearth tax returns of 1665 when, of 36 houses in the village, 23 had only one hearth and another seven had two. At the other end of the social scale were the rector, the lord of the manor,

105 Below, Landownership.
106 Roberts, *Hampshire Houses*, 133.
107 Ibid., 15.
108 NHLE, no. 1302418, Well Ho. (accessed 16 Dec. 2021).
109 NHLE, no. 1339505, Wellhead (accessed 8 Feb. 2022).
110 Below, Landownership.

Figure 5 *The Nook, dated by dendrochronology to 1420–4.*

Figure 6 *Lime Tree Cottage, a medieval cruck-framed building.*

Figure 7 *Bishops Cottage, thought to have been built c.1500.*

Figure 8 *Well House, fronting The Drove with the wellhead adjacent to the left.*

Figure 9 *Ivy and Stable Cottages showing coach entrance (later blocked) to Manor Farm buildings.*

the owner of the Grange and one other with between four and seven hearths.[111] New agricultural methods, and especially the enclosure of Dummer's open fields in 1743 may have helped to widen the social gap in village society. As elsewhere, small landholders lost their access to common pasture and often became landless labourers, while men with capital could accumulate larger acreages in order to farm more profitably. These larger farms required substantial farmhouses and farm yards. Manor Farm House was partly remodelled in the 18th century. It has a courtyard of farm buildings which, it would seem, was formerly accessed through a pretty, 18th-century entrance building, now containing two cottages known as Ivy Cottage and Stable Cottage.[112]

Village Farm House in Up Street is of typical 18th-century form, with chimneys at both ends, a central entry and an outshot under a catslide roof. Until the late 20th century, it had its full complement of agricultural buildings in the farmyard to the rear.[113] These have been redeveloped as a small residential development known, appropriately, as The Barns. A similar development has taken place at Manor Farm in what was the dairy yard. Little Manor Farm House on Down Street dates from the early 19th century.[114]

111 *Hearth Tax 1665*, 218; J. Hare, 'Dummer, Nately Scures and beyond: using the hearth tax assessments of 1665', *Newsletter Hants. F.C.*, 75 (2021), 8–10.
112 NHLE, no. 1093017, Manor Farmho. (accessed 16 Dec. 2021).
113 NHLE, no. 1302412, Village Farmho. (accessed 16 Dec. 2021).
114 NHLE, no. 1093014, Little Manor Farmho. (accessed 16 Dec. 2021).

Figure 10 *Tower Hill Farm House, 1926.*

Tower Hill Farm House, standing at the top of Up Street, probably went through a major re-ordering in the 18th century when the house was largely encased in brick. It seems to have already been a significant farmstead by this date because the core of the house is timber-framed and probably dates from the 17th century. A three-bay timber-framed barn with aisles on three sides probably also dates from this century. It seems to have lost at least one of its original bays and was probably once aisled all around, a form commonly found in the 17th century. There is also a 19th-century granary.[115]

Perhaps the most remarkable small house from the 18th century is Foundry House, which has a dated panel for 1772. It has decorative features including panels of blue-brick headers.[116] Just as the farmhouses reflect change in the agricultural economy, so Foundry House may reflect the coming industrial change rather than merely the presence of a prosperous village blacksmith.

Of the larger houses in the village, the relative grandeur of Dummer House, the Old Rectory[117] and Dummer Down Farm House can be contrasted with the more modest vernacular houses.[118] At the socially lower level in the 19th century the little terrace built as three two-up/two-down cottages and known as Tower Hill Cottages and the similar small terrace at Mount Pleasant on Down Street were probably the homes of landless

115 NHLE, nos 1093016, Tower Hill Fm; 1178466, Granary at Tower Hill Fm (accessed 16 Dec. 2021); HRO, 64M99/B255.
116 NHLE, no. 1302404, Foundry Ho. (accessed 16 Dec. 2021); below, Economic History.
117 Below, Religious History.
118 Below, Landownership, Religious History.

labourers.[119] At a similar scale is the attractive little late 19th-century cottage with a cruciform plan on Farleigh Lane. It has the appearance of a typical lodge building for a large house. It was described as the lodge in 1876 when the main entrance to Dummer House lay here.[120]

Modern Development

As Dummer lost its purely agricultural base, its relatively loose framework was gradually infilled. It became a commuter and retirement village, with older cottages being refurbished and infilling taking place in the form of single dwellings. The latter have both enlarged the perimeter of the built-up area and filled in some of the gaps. However, two significant groupings of local authority dwellings are located at the south-western and north-eastern extremities of the village respectively. The western group, comprising terraced and semi-detached two-storey houses and known as Bible Fields, is located at the top of Dummer Down Lane. It dates from the 1950s.[121] At the other end of the village lies Chapel Close, built in 1948.[122] In addition there are eight old-people's bungalows in Glebe Close (c.1968) and Porter's Close. Despite their uniformity of design, none of these developments is at all particularly conspicuous in the street scene. In 2020 Chapel Close was screened by trees, Porter's Close is largely hidden behind traditional buildings and the Glebe Close properties are sited in a cul-de-sac which extends a little way off Down Street. As a result, the entrance to the village is dominated by traditional buildings and by one of the original village well coverings re-erected on a small green, with a seat under it, to commemorate the Coronation of George VI in 1937.

Kempshott

After Kempshott was incorporated into Winslade in 1393, settlement consisted of little more than a few isolated farms. The former parish was transformed by the building of Kempshott House c.1773, and its continued use as a major household including by the future George IV when Prince of Wales (1788–95).[123] Of the two farmhouses, Southwood Farm may have been built during the first half of the 18th century. It is believed to have been leased by the Prince of Wales for Maria Fitzherbert in 1790 and is a two-storey brick building with attic, a tiled roof with flanking chimneys, a three-bay cast front with two three-light hipped dormer windows and a first-floor band. The only alterations appear to be to the windows, which have 19th-century lights.[124] Kennel farmhouse, originally known as Kempshott farmhouse, the home farm, is an early 19th-century house with later additions.

After the break-up of the Kempshott and Dummer estate in 1926 a section of the park became a golf course. From 2001 housing development took place as part of the Beggarwood estate, transferring to Basingstoke in 2003.[125] The golf course had also been identified for housing as part of the Basingstoke and Deane Local Plan (adopted 2016).[126]

119 NHLE, no. 1178452, Mount Pleasant (accessed 16 Dec. 2021).
120 HRO, M57/SP 373.
121 HRO, H/SY/B1/A12/1.
122 Ibid.; HRO, 128M96/C3/19.
123 Below, Landownership.
124 Golding, *Kempshot Manor*, 8.
125 *Basingstoke and Deane (Parishes) Order* 2003, no. 846.
126 *Basingstoke and Deane Local Plan 2011–2029* (adopted 2016).

Figure 11 *Southwood Farm House in 1926, with single-storey dairy on left of picture.*

Figure 12 *Kennel Farm House showing original early 19th-century house, later two-storey addition to right of picture and single-storey dairy on left.*

IN THE DOMESDAY SURVEY OF 1086, there were two manors, each with its own church and five hides. One, East Dummer, belonged to the de Ports of Basing, from whom the overlordship descended to the St Johns and then the Paulets, the family who dominated north-east Hampshire until the 17th century and beyond. The second manor was held by the Dummer family and then the Pophams, with its overlordship belonging first to the honor of St Valery and then to that of Wallingford, part of the possessions of the crown. In addition, land granted to Waverley Abbey (Surr.) in the late 12th century became Dummer Grange. The manor of Kempshott initially lay outside Dummer parish but eventually became part of it. Although Kempshott shared the same overlord as West Dummer, the de Port lords of Basing and their successors, more importantly it shared a common lord of the manor, and patronage of the church, with Winslade (the Tichbornes). Kempshott had few parishioners before the Black Death and by 1393 it was stated to have none. The parish was therefore merged not with the adjacent Dummer but with the physically separate parish of Winslade. Subsequently, Kempshott's population consisted largely of the manorial household and the related farms. It therefore seemed logical to detach it from Winslade and to link it to Dummer, as occurred in 1879, by which time they also shared a common lord. The lords of Kempshott had already looked towards Dummer and its church from the end of the 18th century, as with the Crookes and Blunts.[2]

The histories of these different properties were often intertwined, two or more units being held under single ownership and then broken up. The two main Dummer manors and their two churches (East and West) seem to have come together after Domesday, and then split. This would have helped to account for the early and undocumented loss of the second Dummer church and the subsequent shared patronage between the lords of the two manors. By the end of the 16th century, the two Dummer manors were united with Dummer Grange in the hands of the Millingates. Later Kempshott and then Dummer (East and West) were all acquired by the Rycrofts. The Kempshott and Dummer estate was broken up by sale in 1926. The major landowners in 2020 included Charles Palmer-Tomkinson (at Dummer Grange), Andrew Ferguson (at Dummer Down Farm) and Alan Hutton of Mapledurwell.

---

1   This chapter is by John Hare, the section on manorial descent on Kempshott by Daniel Spencer with passages on the buildings by Bill Fergie and Edward Roberts.
2   Below, Social History.

Manors

East Dummer

What became known in the 16th century as *East Dummer* or *Popham Dummer* was probably the five hides of land in Dummer held by Oda of Winchester and his tenant Hunger in 1086, which in 1066 had been held by Auti from King Edward.[3] Oda's lands subsequently became part of the honor of St Valery, which later escheated to the crown in the reign of Henry III.[4] It was regranted by that king to his brother Richard, earl of Cornwall. On the death of Richard's son Edmund without heirs, his estates, including the honors of St Valery and Wallingford, once more came into the king's hands.[5] Subsequently, the overlordship of Dummer was transferred to the royal honor of Wallingford.[6]

In 1086, a certain Hunger held these five hides as a sub-tenant of Oda. Three 'hagae' in Winchester which paid a rent of 2*s.* were annexed to the property.[7] It is possible that this Hunger may have been the ancestor of the Dummer family, noted in the later Winchester surveys. In *c*.1110, Henry of Dummer possessed rents from three properties in Winchester, possibly the three 'hagae' of Domesday Book, and in 1148 Ralph of Dummer held lands in Tanner Street, Winchester.[8] He was probably the Ralph de Dummer who held West Dummer in 1165/6, so bringing together the two manors and parishes.[9] In 1198 his son Robert gave half a hide of land in Dummer to his brother Geoffrey, parson of the church,[10] and it may be assumed that the property in Dummer passed through his son Richard, who was living in 1248,[11] to John Dummer of Easton (Leics.), who agreed with the lord of the West manor to the alternate presentation to the rectory in 1275 and who died in possession of the manors of Dummer and Easton in 1304.[12] He was succeeded by Robert, his son and heir, in 1308, who also held land in Watford (Northants.).[13] Robert presented to the church in 1304 and 1330, held the manor in 1316 and died in 1336.[14] He was succeeded by his daughter Alice and her husband John Astwick (of Astwick, Beds.), who was also bailiff of Gartree hundred (Leics.).[15] This

---

3   *Domesday*, 121.
4   *Cal. Inq. p.m.* I, no. 808.
5   *Cal. Inq. p.m.* III, no. 604.
6   *Cal. Inq. p.m.* XVII, no. 1073.
7   Auti also held Ellisfield: *PASE Domesday*, s.v. 'Auti 3': https://domesday.pase.ac.uk/ (accessed 21 Jan. 2022); *VCH Hants.* III, 360; *Domesday*, 121.
8   F. Barlow, M. Biddle, D. von Feilitzen and D.J. Keene, *Winchester in the Early Middle Ages* (Oxford, 1976), 35, 48, 54, 115.
9   Below, West Dummer.
10   *Feet of Fines 10 Ric. I* (PRS, 24), no. 144, 97.
11   *Feudal Aids* II, 330.
12   *Cal. Inq. p.m.* IV, no. 195; *VCH Leics.* V, 53.
13   *Cal. Inq. p.m.* IV, no. 356. One unresolved complication is provided by an Inquisition Post Mortem for John de Dummer, who held land in Easton and Dummer as well as land in Watford (Northants.), but whose heir was not his son Robert aged 28 (1304), but Richard aged 18 (1308).
14   *Feudal Aids* II, 313; *VCH Leics.* V, 53, *Reg. Pontissara*, I, 177; *Reg. Stratford*, I, 381.
15   *VCH Beds.* II, 203; *VCH Leics.* V, 53.

John presented to Dummer rectory in 1342/3 and held the manor in 1346.[16] He appears
to have been a 'King's merchant', engaged in royal business in various parts of England,
and when summoned to appear before the council at Westminster, sought protection
on the ground that he was liable to be seized on account of certain debts.[17] He was
succeeded c.1346 by his son John, whose daughter Agnes married John de Drayton, and
in 1368–9 they conveyed all their rights in the manor of Dummer to Sir John Popham of
the adjoining hamlet of Popham.[18]

The Pophams were an influential family within the county gentry community,
providing representatives for the county to over a score of 14th-century parliaments.[19]
From Sir John, it passed to Philip Popham, possibly a younger son, and Elizabeth
his wife. They were succeeded in 1397 by a second Philip and Elizabeth.[20] The latter
survived her husband until 1408,[21] and (her son Philip having died) left as coheiresses
two sisters, Margaret and Matilda, aged 14 and 13 years.[22] Both girls had been married
or betrothed to John and Peter Cowdray, members of another prominent county gentry
family based at Herriard.[23] Dummer seems to have been initially allotted to Matilda.[24] It
then passed to her sister, who married as her second husband Edward Wayte of Draycot
Cerne (Wilts.),[25] and thirdly Robert Long of South Wraxall (Wilts.), who held one fee in
Dummer in 1428,[26] and was succeeded by his son John, who had married his stepsister
Margaret Wayte, heiress of the Wayte family, and held the manor in 1483.[27] John was
followed by Thomas Long, who presented to the rectory in 1488, and Henry Long, who
presented in 1509.[28]

The next century saw further change in ownership. In 1529 Robert Drury and
Alice his wife quitclaimed the manor of Dummer to William Barentyne.[29] It passed by
fine from Walter Bonham and Alice, daughter of John Dale to William Dale, the latter
holding East manor from at least 1546/7 to at least 1564.[30] In 1577 it passed from Richard
Kingsmill and Robert Brinnage to Nicholas Venables of Andover, gent. John Millingate
acquired the manor in 1583[31] and by 1593 he was in possession of both manors and
Dummer Grange.[32]

The identity of John Millingate is complicated by the presence of three or four
successive John Millingates. We know little of their origins although they were probably

16   Reg. Pontissara, I, 177; *Feudal Aids* II, 330.
17   *Cal. Pat.* 1343–5, 226; 1345–8, 248, 273.
18   *VCH Beds.* II, 203–4; *Cal. Close*, 1364–69, 74–5; 'dated at their manor of Dumere'.
19   J.S. Roskell, 'Sir John Popham, Knight Banneret of Charford', *Proc. Hants. F.C.*, 21 (1958), 40.
20   *Cal. Inq. p.m.* XVII, no. 1073.
21   *Cal. Inq. p.m.* XIX, no. 369.
22   *Cal. Inq. p.m.* XIX, no. 369; XX, no. 273.
23   *Cal. Inq. p.m.* XX, no. 165.
24   HRO, 44M69/C524.
25   W. Chitty, *Historical Account of the Family of Long of Wiltshire* (London, 1889), 14; *Cal. Inq. p.m.* XXXV, no. 3.
26   *Feudal Aids* II, 344 (lately John Astewyk), 364.
27   Chitty, *Long*, 16; *Hist. Parl.* 1422–61, VII, 298–300.
28   Reg. Fox I, 15, 19d.; P.M. Slocombe, *Whaddon and the Longs* (Gloucester, 2020), 45, 47.
29   *VCH Hants.* III, 360.
30   HRO, 55M67/E1; 55M67/M19.
31   HRO, 41M77/139/4.
32   Below, Dummer Grange.

from nearby Northington or East Stratton (now included in Micheldever parish).[33] John acquired Dummer Grange in 1579/80. In 1586 John Millingate the elder was one of the two most highly assessed figures in terms of goods (although, significantly, not on land) and John Millingate the younger was also a well-off figure.[34] By 1583, John (probably the elder) had acquired the East manor, and in 1593 the West manor. He was wealthy enough to provide the church with three bells.[35] By 1597 both courts were held in his name.[36] Nevertheless, the family kept their main home at the Grange, and in 1626 and 1632 John Millingate, father and then son, were in turn described as of the Grange Dummer.[37] A John Millingate died in 1626, leaving a son and grandchildren, with a John in each generation.[38] At the death of the last John in 1655, most of his lands passed to his daughter Joan and her children. Her husband, Mathew Terry, was already dead, as was her brother, John.[39] Joan was thus the beneficiary of both her father's and brother's wills. Their wills, moreover, reflect something of the changing world of this family. The first John had evidently achieved wealth and became a landowner. His son, or grandson, was similarly established but in 1626 was apparently illiterate: he used his mark on his will.[40] Despite this he was concerned with education and endowed the village's first school.[41] By contrast his son, who died in 1641, left behind a series of books on law, arithmetic, two dictionaries, Smith's *Sermons*, two Bibles and the *Practice of Piety*, as well as the accoutrements of gentility, a fowling piece and a rapier.[42] The Millingates remained in possession until the middle of the 17th century, when the main manors passed into the Terry family as a result of the marriage of Joan Millingate to Mathew Terry.[43] The Terry family continued to dominate Dummer as the parish's principal landowners for the succeeding two centuries, as with Thomas Terry and his son Stephen, the diarist. Despite the family having sold Dummer Grange, Stephen still held 63 per cent of the land assessed for tithe in 1840.[44] In 1864−5, the manor house and a considerable part of the parish was sold to Revd Thomas Torr,[45] and in 1876, they were sold to Sir Nelson Rycroft, Bt,[46] whose son, Sir Richard Nelson Rycroft, Bt, succeeded as lord of the manor in 1894.[47] The estate was broken up by sale in 1926, although his son remained living in Dummer House.[48]

33   HRO, 41M77/139/4: John, son of Robert Millingate was baptised in 1538.
34   *Hants. Lay Subsidy 1586*, 54.
35   Below, Religious History.
36   HRO, 55M67/M4.
37   HRO, 13M64/57; 1626B/084; 44M69/D12/4/125.
38   HRO, 13M64/57; 1626B/084. A family tree compiled in 1887 in the family collection suggests that there was an additional generation including another John, and that one of the Johns of 1586 was already dead (HRO, 9M69/4).
39   HRO, 1641A/078.
40   HRO, 13M64/57; 1626B/084.
41   Below, Education.
42   HRO, 1641A/078.
43   HRO, 1641A/078.
44   HRO, 21M65/F7/64/1.
45   BL, 004830987; HRO, 55M67/T7.
46   HRO, 10M57/SP373.
47   *The Times*, Obituary, 7 Oct. 1925.
48   HRO, 87M99/5; *Kelly's Dir. Hants.* 1931, 182.

Figure 13 *Stephen Terry in his 91st year.*

Dummer House represents the manor house and occupies an important site at the centre of the village, close to the church and Manor Farm. In this location it is likely that it is the latest in a sequence of manor houses dating back to the Middle Ages: in 1304 it possessed a hall roofed with thatch, a barn, a decayed oxshed and buildings.[49] In 1665, the predecessor of the present house was probably represented by the second largest house in the village, that of the Terrys, with its six hearths in 1665.[50] The present house dates from the 18th and 19th centuries, and if it incorporates earlier fabric this is not obvious from either the interior or the exterior. It was formerly early Georgian, but was remodelled and considerably extended in the early 19th century. It is stuccoed and the main elevation is of 11 bays. The present façade is shown in the sale particulars of 1876, although without the later porch,[51] and was probably in place by 1845 since it is shown in a photograph affixed in Terry's diary for that year.[52] The central five bays project slightly and are emphasised by the pediment above. The rear elevation is of seven bays, of which the four to the left date from the 18th century and the remainder to the 19th century. In the interior the entrance hall

49   TNA, C 133/111/8.
50   *Hearth Tax 1665*, 218.
51   HRO, 10M57/SP373.
52   HRO, 24M49/5.

Figure 14 *Dummer House, repro print from 1876.*

has a low, deeply coffered ceiling and a square 18th-century stairwell with tapered square section balusters. At first-floor level three painted early 17th-century panels are clearly *ex situ* and perhaps point to an earlier house.[53]

West Dummer, or De Port, St John and Paulet manor

The manor known in the 16th century as West Dummer was probably the five hides of land held at the time of the Domesday survey by one of the men of Hugh de Port, the dominant landowner in north-east Hampshire. Alric had held it from King Edward.[54] Although stripped of his estates in Hampshire, Alric apparently survived the Conquest and may be identified as the tenant-in-chief of Nettlestone and Sheat (probably in Gatcombe) on the Isle of Wight which he held both in 1066 and 1086.[55] The overlordship of this manor passed with that of Hugh's other estates to his descendants, the St Johns and Paulets of Basing.[56]

The first mention of a tenant of the De Ports in Dummer after the time of the Domesday survey occurs early in the 13th century, when William Dummer was called

53   Pevsner, *North Hampshire*, 240; NHLE, no. 1093020 Dummer Ho. (accessed 16 Dec. 2021).
54   *Domesday*, 108.
55   *PASE Domesday*, s.v. 'Alric 11': https://domesday.pase.ac.uk/ (accessed 21 Jan. 2022); *VCH Hants.* V, 189, 246; *Domesday*, 133.
56   As in 1360, *Cal. Inq. p.m.* IX, Ed. III, 29–43.

upon to do homage for two knights' fees in Dummer.[57] But in 1165/6 Ralph de Dummer had married Agnes, who brought with her the manor of Penne (Pendomer, Somt) which the family retained until the early 14th century.[58] This was probably the Ralph of Dummer who held the East Dummer manor in 1148. This common ownership may have resulted in the shared advowson of the church and the loss of one of the two churches suggested by the Domesday survey.[59] In 1294–5 the abbot of Waverley recovered possession against John, son of William Dummer, in a dispute over the right of common pasture in Dummer, which the abbot alleged belonged to his free tenement.[60] Sir John Dummer was a man of considerable importance in Somerset, representing it in the parliaments of 1306 and 1313.[61] He held Dummer as well as his Somerset lands in 1303 but died by 1304.[62] He was probably the same John Dummer referred to in 1289 when the sheriff of Somerset was ordered to elect a new coroner in place of John de Dummer because he was of the household of John de St John, who was then with the king.[63] In 1316 Thomas, son of Sir John Dummer held one half of the vill of Dummer.[64] From Thomas the estate passed to his son, also Thomas, who held it in 1329 and again in 1346.[65] He appears to have been the last male heir of the family. This would explain the next two lords, representing marriage to the heiress. Robert Wynegod presented to the rectory in 1330, while John Wynegod held two fees here in 1360, and had presented in 1344.[66] Their tenure, however, was short-lived and a new heiress, or widow, Ellen, married Nicholas atte More. Her descendants assumed the name of Dummer,[67] and held the manor until the death of William Dummer in 1593. Henry Dommere held a fee in 1428,[68] his son, Robert, presented to the rectory in 1450, 1453 and 1462,[69] another Henry in 1509 and Richard (Robert's grandson) in 1524–5.[70] Henry Dummer possessed the manor in 1540, followed by William Dummer who presented in 1564.[71] The latter held his first court here in 1537, and he or a son was still holding one in 1583, while in 1584 George Wither described him as 'my beloved landlord'.[72] In 1579, however, William, who had married Katherine Brydges, granted the reversion to Humphrey Brydges, of

57   T. Bond, 'Pendomer, co. Somerset', in *Proc. of Somerset Archaeological and Natural Hist. Soc.*, 17 (1871), 95; *Placit. in Domo Capit. Abbrev.*, 73b.
58   Bond, 'Pendomer', 95–108.
59   Above, East manor; below, Religious History.
60   *Abbrev. Rot. Orig.*, 91.
61   *Parl. Writs* I, p. xxviii.
62   Bond, 'Pendomer', 100; *Cal. Inq. p.m.* IV, 123, 276.
63   *Cal. Close*, 1288–96, p. 25.
64   TNA, CP 40/236, m. 332; *Feudal Aids* II, 313; *Reg. Woodlock* II, 744.
65   *Cal. Inq. p.m.* VII, no. 244; *Feudal Aids* II, 330. This leaves unresolved the issue of the presentments to the rectory in 1330 and 1345 by members of the Wynegod family. Could this have been the result of Thomas granting the manor to his daughter during his lifetime?
66   *Cal. Inq. p.m.* IX, no. 52 (and specifically held from the St John barony); *Reg. Stratford* I, 439.
67   *VCH Hants.* III, 1541; following Bond, 'Pendomer', makes her the daughter of Thomas de Dummer. It is therefore not clear whether Ellen was the wife of Robert Wynegod or of Nicholas atte More. The church includes a brass of 1427 to William Dummer – perhaps a younger brother – and his wife Elena.
68   *Feudal Aids* II, 344 lately Thomas de Dommer.
69   Reg. Waynflete I, 28v.; I 59v.; I 119.
70   Reg. Fox V, 98 and 154, and below, Religious History.
71   HRO, 1540B/26; Reg. Horne, 9.
72   HRO, 55M67/M30, M35; 1586A/89; 312M87/E10/1.

Lincolns Inn, William's steward and probably Katherine's brother, with reversion to John Millingate, and in 1586 the manor was conveyed by fine from Humphrey Brydges to John.[73] William died in 1593 and by 1597 both courts for the East and West manor were held for John Millingate.[74] Thereafter the two manors remained in the same hands, from Millingate to Terrys and to Rycrofts. West Dummer descended with East Dummer.

The site of the west manor house is unclear, although the focus of the manor was probably on the junction of Up Street and Dummer Down Lane. Dummer Down Farm House seems to have been the largest house and may represent its successor, although it does not seem to have existed at the time of the enclosure in 1743, and its isolated location gave it a central position for a group of new enclosed fields.[75] A chief messuage remained despite the common ownership of the two manors.[76] The present house dates from the 18th century with 19th-century and later alterations and additions. It is built of brick in English bond and has a well-proportioned, symmetrical, south-east front of three bays. It is of two storeys with an attic lit by a central hipped dormer. The ground floor windows have rubbed brick flat arches and stone cills. There is a lead cistern in the garden with the date 1704, but this was possibly associated with an earlier house elsewhere.[77]

Figure 15 *Dummer Down Farm House in 1951.*

73   TNA, CP 25/210. It may be that Nicholas Venables conveyed half the manor by fine to John Millingate in
      1591; *VCH Hants.* III, 358, ascribed this to East manor but this was already in Millingate's hands by 1583.
74   HRO, 55M67/M4.
75   HRO, 10M57/A7/1.
76   HRO, 55M67/T17.
77   NHLE, no. 1302386, Dummer Down Farmho. (accessed 16 Dec. 2021).

Dummer Grange

The grant of land to Waverley Abbey, the first Cistercian monastery to be founded in England, formed the basis of the small Dummer Grange. It was not in a list of the abbey's property in 1147, but had been acquired by 1181[78] and was afterwards confirmed by charters of King John and Edward II.[79] It was valued at £2 in 1291.[80] Its grant and probable expansion led to conflict with the rector of Dummer over tithes in 1276 and with the lord of Dummer over rights of common in 1294–5.[81] The Grange remained in the abbey's possession until the latter's suppression in 1536[82] and was valued at £2 10s. in 1535.[83] In the following year the abbey and its lands were granted to Sir William Fitz William, a leading soldier, courtier and minister under Henry VIII, who was rewarded with the title of earl of Southampton.[84] At his death in 1542, his lands passed to his half-brother Sir Anthony Browne and the latter's son Viscount Montague, who held Dummer in 1566 when it was leased from him and in turn was sublet by Nicholas Madgwick.[85] In 1579/80, it was acquired by John Millingate, his first substantial holding in the village,[86] and it subsequently remained the family's chief residence, John Millingate being described as of the Grange at Dummer in 1626 and 1632.[87] After the death of the last John Millingate in 1655,[88] the estate was broken up. The Dummer manors passed to his eldest daughter, Joanne, and to the Terry family, but the Grange remained with his widow and after her death (in 1659) it passed to another daughter, Amy, who had married William Soper, from another leading family in the village.[89] The Millingates, and possibly the Sopers, made substantial additions to the house. It remained with the Sopers until 1729, when John Soper of Preston Candover left it to his second daughter, Elizabeth.[90] At her death it fell to her sister, Frances, who married George Garnier in 1736.[91] She died in 1739, and shortly after, it was acquired by the Michael Terry, who had married the eldest of the three Soper sisters. He held it in the Enclosure Act of 1734[92] and later leased it to

78   Service, *Waverley Abbey*, 228, 237.

79   Chart R (Rec. Com.) 7 John, 161, Cal. Char, III, 372–3.

80   *Tax Eccl.,* 215.

81   E. Sussex. RO, BAT/4/6/1406 (Catalogue).

82   *L&P Hen. VIII*, XL, 372–3.

83   *Valor Eccl. II*, 35.

84   *Hist. Parl.* 1509–58, s.v. FitzWilliam, Sir William I (*c.*1490–1542) of Cowdray, Sussex and London (accessed 1 Mar. 2022); Service, *Waverley Abbey*, 252.

85   TNA, PROB 11/48/417.

86   TNA, CP 26/2/209/22ELIZIHIL m. 38.

87   HRO, 13M64/57; 1626B/084; 44M69/D12/4/125; 44M69/D1/85/5.

88   TNA, PROB 11/252/375.

89   TNA, PROB 11/292/246.

90   TNA, PROB 11/633/139. It was held by Richard Soper in 1712 (TNA, PROB 11/633/139; PROB 12/58/57).

91   R. Andreae, *Huguenots, Apothecaries, Gardeners and Squires: the Garniers of Rookesbury* (Winchester, 2021), 9.

92   From the monastic grange onwards, the estate would have included land within the open fields for which the owner would receive compensation at enclosure as well as enclosed fields colonised from the downs. Most of the Grange's land lay outside the enclosure agreement but there was also a new enclosed field that belonged to Grange farm.

Figure 16 *Dummer Grange, 1930s, by E.S. McEuen.*

a tenant in 1752.[93] By 1803 it belonged to William Heath, followed by Thomas Heath by 1820.[94] It was sold in 1829, together with the advowson, probably to Dr William Adams, who held it by 1832[95] and who held 276 a. in the tithe assessment returns of 1838/40. No house was then mentioned, but the outline of the original estate can still be seen in the tithe map of 1840.[96] Adams was a London lawyer, of Thorpe, Surrey, later specified as 'of The Grange, Dummer'. He presented his son, William Cockayne Adams, to the rectory in 1848, and probably built the new rectory for him in 1850. His son Borlase Hill Adams (d. 1885) presented to the rectory in 1875 and 1881/2, and in 1878 he, then living at the Grange, was involved in an exchange over tithes.[97] The property was put up for sale in 1881 by Mr Eiloart.[98] Robert Miller held the Grange in the 1920s.[99] Dummer Grange was bought by the family of the present owner, Charles Palmer-Tomkinson, in 1950.[100]

Dummer Grange itself, is the finest 17th-century house in the parish, with walls made entirely from brick. The hall range was built about 1600 by John Millingate. It contrasts with the more elaborate, and later, south wing with its richly moulded brickwork with classical motifs in the Artisan Mannerist style.[101] This style, with its application of classical architectural features, was especially popular with lesser country gentry in the years in and around the third quarter of the 17th century, a period when the Millingate and

93   HRO, 55M67/T16.
94   HRO, Q22/1/1/147.
95   HRO, 10M57/SP 365.
96   HRO, 21M65/F7/64/2.
97   HRO, 34M95/2.
98   HRO, 10M57/SP374.
99   *Kelly's Dir. Hants.* 1920, 108; *Kelly's Dir. Hants.* 1923, 189; *Kelly's Dir. Hants.* 1927, 134; *Kelly's Dir. Hants.* 1931, 182.
100 HRO, 5M70/27.
101 Pevsner, *North Hampshire*, 240; NHLE, no. 1339510, Dummer Grange (accessed 16 Dec. 2021).

Soper families were living at the Grange. The enlarged house could have been the work of William Soper after he acquired the Grange in 1659, and was probably complete by 1665 when Soper's house had seven hearths, the largest number in the parish.[102] This proliferation was reflected in the rooms and fireplaces recorded in subsequent inventories in 1688 and 1701.[103] The north-east wing of the house replaced a smaller earlier structure and was built in a similar style in the early 20th century, by Robert Miller.[104]

Kempshott

The Domesday survey states that by 1086 Kempshott was held by Walter of Hugh de Port and before the Norman Conquest by Ealdraed.[105] In 1256, the manor was recorded as being held by Hugh de Sifrewast of Reginald Fitz Peter for half a knight's fee.[106] Kempshott remained in the possession of the Sifrewast family until the early 14th century, when it was inherited by Margaret, daughter and heir of Roger de Sifrewast. John Tichborne was then able to acquire the manor as part of his marriage settlement with Margaret and was recorded as being lord of the manor in 1316.[107] His successor Roger de Tycheborne held it in 1346.[108] The Tichbornes held Tichborne near Alresford in mid Hampshire from the 12th century and owned other land in north Hampshire including Winslade, a few miles from Kempshott, and the advowsons of both Kempshott and Winslade. This led to the parishes being joined in 1393, when Kempshott had no resident population.[109]

Kempshott remained in the possession of the Tichborne family until 1578, when it was sold by Benjamin Tichborne to Henry Pinck(e), a yeoman who lived and farmed there for the following 33 years.[110] Upon the death of Henry Pinck in 1611, the manor passed to his son, Robert Pinck, a senior proctor of New College, Oxford. Yet Robert's successful university career meant that he continued to reside in Oxford after this date, where he was elected as warden of New College in 1617. His support for the king during the early stages of the Civil Wars, which included mustering and drilling the scholars of the college, led to his imprisonment by the parliamentarians from 12 September 1642 to 5 January 1643.[111] Robert died on 2 November 1647, and by a will dated 22 May of the same year, left Kempshott to his nephew Henry Pinck of North Waltham.[112] Henry was succeeded by his son, Thomas Pinck (d. 1708), who served as mayor of Winchester

---

102 *Hearth Tax*, 218.
103 TNA, PROB 4/3197; HRO, 1701A/093.
104 A newspaper report on a Hampshire Field Club meeting at Dummer in 1949 states that it was built in 1914 by Robert Miller. There may have been several phases in this work, as shown in a photograph taken in 1911 (HRO, DC/L6/4/2/6, 8). This shows the new north-east wing but not the porch which incorporates a coat of arms with the date 1920.
105 *Domesday*, 107.
106 TNA, JUST 1/778.
107 Toby Scott Purser, 'The County Community of Hampshire, *c.*1300–*c.*1530, With Special Reference to the Knights and Esquires' (unpubl. PhD thesis, Univ. of Southampton (Winchester), 2001), 104.
108 *Feudal Aids* II, 332.
109 *Reg. Wykeham* II, 441–3.
110 HRO, 25M55/95; 1611A/079.
111 *ODNB*, s.v. Pinck, Robert (bap. 1573, d. 1647) (accessed 23 Mar. 2017).
112 Ibid.

1689–90.[113] The estate then passed to the latter's son, Revd Henry Pinck, vicar of South Damerham (Wilts., now Hants.), until his death in 1723, when he was succeeded in turn by his son, Henry Pinck.[114] Henry died in 1770 and in his will left the estate to his niece Dorothy, wife of John Lee of Woolley Firs (Berks.).[115]

The manor was subsequently sold to Philip Dehany, esquire, tenant of Farleigh House, Farleigh Wallop, who in 1773 knocked down the farmhouse and 'built a large mansion of plain exterior, but handsome and commodious within'.[116] Philip Dehany was the son of David Dehany, a Bristol merchant who owned sugar estates in Jamaica and Barbados.[117] Philip possessed property in Kent, London and Hampshire, where his friendship with the Duke of Bolton at Hackwood may have influenced his choice to settle in the neighbourhood.[118]

James Morley, an East India Company merchant, purchased the estate in 1787 but on the death of his wife sold it in the following year to John Crosse Crooke Esq.[119] Crooke was leasing nearby Stratton Park and did not occupy Kempshott House until later in his

Figure 17 *Kempshott Park, lithograph by G.F. Prosser, Select Views of Hampshire, 1833.*

113 *VCH Hants.* IV, 179–80.

114 Misc. Gen. et Her. (Ser. 3), II, 105–12; HRO, 55M67/T144.

115 HRO, 55M67/T149–54.

116 HRO, 55M67/T157–9; Golding, *Kempshot Manor*, 4; *Cliddesden*, 102.

117 *Legacies of British Slave Ownership Database*, s.v. 'Philip Dehany': http://wwwdepts-live.ucl.ac.uk/lbs/person/view/2146638189/ (accessed 20 May 2020).

118 *Hist. Parl.* 1754–90, s.v. Dehany, Philip (*c.*1720–1809) of Queen Anne St., London and Hayes Pl. Kent. (accessed 20 May 2020).

119 HRO, 55M67/T171–3; T177–9; www.kempshottmanor.net/ (accessed 1 Feb. 2020).

life. Indeed, from 1789 to 1795 he leased the manor to George Augustus Frederick, the Prince of Wales and future George IV, as a hunting lodge. The prince spent large sums on improving the house and its furnishings to suit the needs of a royal residence and added stables and kennels. He oversaw the creation of the park from plans probably commissioned by John Crooke.[120] The estate was subsequently leased by Guy Carleton, 1st baron Dorchester, from 1796 to 1803.[121] Carleton's career had been in Canada as a general and twice governor of Quebec. He retired to England in 1796 to the life of a country squire. He had already bought the nearby manor of Nately Scures, although this lacked the big house Kempshott offered.[122] John Crooke returned in 1803 until his death,[123] and a hatchment in the gallery of Dummer church is dedicated to 'John Crooke of Kempshott Park'. Edward Walter Blunt, Esq. (d. 1860) purchased the manor from Crooke's widow in 1832.

In 1866 Sir Nelson Rycroft purchased Kempshott and subsequently the two Dummer manors, living in the grander house at Kempshott. He was succeeded by his son, Sir Richard Nelson Rycroft, in 1894, who lived in Dummer House and who had leased the Kempshott estate to Henry Gourlay, a shipbuilder from Dundee, between at least 1899 and 1911.[124] His daughter's subsequent success at golf should probably be associated with the conversion of parts of the park into a golf course.[125]

Kempshott was transformed by the destruction of the existing manor house and the building of Kempshott House by Dehany in 1773. It appears typical of many mid to late 18th-century gentry houses, built to impress: a three-storey brick house situated on a small hill to the south of the turnpike road running from Winchester to London surrounded by parkland, and clearly seen by passing travellers. During the time that the Prince of Wales leased Kempshott House (1788–95) alterations and improvements were made probably on the advice of his architect Henry Holland, architect of Brighton Pavilion and of the rebuilding of the prince's Carlton House in London. It is not clear exactly what these changes were. Prosser, writing in 1833, commented that during this period, 'tasteful decorations were added to the interior of the mansion which are still preserved', and some panels by the French painter, Louis Delabrière, who also worked at Carlton House, still survive – albeit in America.[126] What is not clear is whether he expanded the buildings. It may be to the prince's period of occupation that we should ascribe the addition of a pair of curved wings at the rear providing additional offices and rooms. These wings were there by 1795 and remained in 1831.[127] Holland's last proposed enlargements, in 1795, came at the end of the prince's stay there. He moved to the Grange at Northington in the same year, and the changes were not carried out.[128] Prosser, in

120 Above, Introduction; below, Social History.
121 www.kempshottmanor.net/ (accessed 1 Feb. 2020).
122 *ODNB*, s.v. Carleton, Guy. The First Baron Dorchester (accessed 23 Mar. 2017); G. McKelvie, *Nately Scures, Land Ownership, VCH Hants.*, work in progress (accessed 23 Apr. 2017).
123 G. Prosser, *Select Illustrations of Hampshire Comprising Picturesque Views of the Seats of the Nobility and Gentry* (London and Camberwell, 1833).
124 *Kelly's Dir. Hants.* 1899, 140; 1911, 175; *Burke's Peerage* (2003), I, 1287.
125 The presence of an earlier golf course is recorded in the 1926 sale particulars, HRO, 87M99/5.
126 J. Harris, 'The room that never was. Myth of the Kempshott Park Saloon', *Country Life*, 11. Oct. 1988, 260.
127 Reproduced in Golding, *Kempshot Manor*, figs 6, 13, 17, 18 from Royal Collections (R.L. 29634–7); HRO, 10M57/SP368, 369.
128 Reproduced in Golding, *Kempshot Manor*, figs 6, 13, 17, 18.

1833, also refers to the impact of this period on the park when it was replanted under a 'celebrated landscape gardener'.[129]

The exterior of the house was remodelled after 1832 by Blunt, to the designs of the architect Sampson Kempthorne.[130] By 1833 he had cased the now unfashionable brick façade in stucco, and added various pediments and other classical features.[131] Subsequently, probably in 1873, Rycroft considerably enlarged the house, replacing the curved wings by a new higher rear extension which dominated the old core and survived until the destruction of the whole house.[132] At its sale in 1926, the house included six reception rooms and 22 bed and dressing rooms.[133] Then or soon afterwards some of the interior fittings were sold, although the so-called Kempshott Park Saloon in the City Art Museum, St Louis, USA, is no longer seen as coming from here. It contained some Kempshott material – painted panels from around a gallery to the staircase and a mantelpiece – but mixed together with fittings from other houses and imaginative reconstructions.[134]

After the death of Gourlay in 1915, the house was never again to be a family seat. It served a variety of other purposes and saw a long, drawn-out process of decline in the 20th century. It provided accommodation for German prisoners of war who worked on local farms[135] and was then converted into flats.[136] In the Second World War the house and grounds were again requisitioned as the headquarters of the Canadian Petroleum Warfare Experimental Unit, developing and testing flame weapons.[137] In 1949 the house was bought by Harold Hounsome and was used for grain drying and storage.[138] By the 1960s it was in an unsafe condition and demolition was finally completed in 1972 or soon after.[139] In 2020 only the stable block and clock house survived. The park was sold to Basingstoke Golf Club in 1927. Part of the site was developed for housing from 2001, and further expansion of housing was well under way in 2022.[140]

Overview

The accumulated scraps of information have allowed the construction of a picture of landholding in a single Hampshire parish and can reveal something of the varied complexities of English landholding since the Norman Conquest. Many English villages were part of great aristocratic estates belonging to absentee landlords. This was not

129 Prosser, *Select Views of Hampshire*. This may possibly have referred to Repton, who had worked for the prince at Brighton: Golding, *Kempshot Manor*, 5.
130 Prosser ibid.; he subsequently became well known for his designs for Poor Law workhouses, which included that at Old Basing. H.M. Colvin, *A Biographical Dictionary of British Architects, 1600–1840* (New York, 1978), 486–7; B. Large, *Basingstoke Workhouse and Poor Law Union* (Stroud, 2016), 28.
131 Prosser, *Select Views of Hampshire*.
132 *Kelly's Dir. Hants. 1889*, 18 records that it was greatly added to and improved in 1873.
133 HRO, 87M99/5.
134 Harris, 'The room that never was', 260; ibid., 'English rooms in American museums', *Country Life*, 8 June 1961, 1326–7.
135 Napier, *Kempshott Park*, 13.
136 Ibid; *Kelly's Dir. Hants. 1923*, 189.
137 Napier, *Kempshott Park*, 17.
138 He already owned the petrol station at the top of Kempshott Hill; below, Economic History.
139 Napier, *Kempshott Park*, 20. Parts remained when the motorway opened in 1971.
140 Above, Introduction; below, Social History.

Figure 18 *Kempshott House, showing the semi-circular bows rising to the full height of the house, the semi-circular loggia of paired columns and the post-1832 stuccoed façade.*

the case in Dummer. Here the lords were usually local and resident, as evident from Margaret Popham's christening in 1400 to William Dummer's burial in 1593. Later, the residential presence here of the Terrys in the late 18th and the 19th centuries is evident in the diaries of Stephen Terry and in the letters of Jane Austen.

The Millingates provide an interesting perspective on this local picture. Coming from a neighbouring village, their rise at the end of the 16th century was dramatic. They quickly built up ownership of the Grange, where they became resident, and then of the East and West manors. Together with their daughters' children, the Sopers and the Terrys, they dominated the landholding of Dummer in an unbroken sequence for almost 300 years. By contrast, new wealth also came into the manors, most dramatically seen in the 18th and 19th centuries and above all in Kempshott, where the short-term owners and inhabitants included the son of a wealthy merchant, a general and colonial governor, and a royal heir to the throne.

The medieval lords of Dummer were generally local gentry with one or two manors and local interests. Nevertheless, sometimes they became more influential within the county community of Hampshire or beyond, as with the Pophams and Sifrewasts, and at various times they held land outside Dummer, in Leicestershire, Northamptonshire, Somerset and Dorset, and played a role elsewhere. Subsequently new entrants might become influential in county politics and administration, as with the Blunts and Rycrofts in the 19th century. Both Rycrofts were high sheriffs of Hampshire in 1881 and 1899, and both were unchallenged as county councillors for Dummer from 1889 to 1923.[141] Later in the 20th century, Nelson Rycroft was sheriff in 1939 and Charles Palmer-Tomkinson in 1994.[142] Occasionally we can see national issues intruding. Mathew Terry fought on the parliamentary side in the 17th-century Civil Wars and was wounded at the battle of Alton, dying soon afterwards. Moreover, Dummer Grange provides a partial contrast to this local picture. During the Middle Ages it was a small peripheral possession of Waverley Abbey (Surr.), and afterwards for a brief time it remained a similar possession of a rich aristocratic family, the Fitzwilliam, earl of Southampton, of Cowdray House (Suss.), and the viscount Montague, of Cowdray and Battle (Suss.), neither of whom is likely to have visited the manor. But later the Grange was absorbed into the pattern of local Dummer landownership under the Millingates, Sopers and Terrys.

Finally, changes can be seen within the relatively stable and often interconnecting structure of these four units of landownership: the coming together of different blocks and then their breaking apart, whether in the 12th century, around 1600, around 1700, or in 1876 and 1926.

141 *Burke's Peerage, Baronetage and Knightage* (1970); R. Ottewill, *Hampshire and Surrey County Council Elections 1889–1974* (Winchester, 2010), Wessex Historical Databases 4, CD Rom.
142 Ibid.; HRO, H/CE3/2/22.

ECONOMIC HISTORY

UNTIL THE MID 20TH CENTURY Dummer and Kempshott's economy was based on agriculture, with most inhabitants engaged in farming or in an associated rural craft or industry. An unusually extensive collection of manorial court records provides a detailed insight into the management of the common agricultural system which existed until parliamentary enclosure of the land in 1743. The enclosure award transformed the common fields and commons and set the pattern of the parish landscape, which was largely unchanged in 2020. Proximity to Basingstoke provided a local market for produce and the main London to Salisbury and Southampton roads which traversed the parish enabled a wider distribution of goods. The woollen industry was important from the Middle Ages, peaking in the early 16th century. An iron foundry existed in the village in the 19th and early 20th centuries. In the 21st century the majority of residents were employed outside the parish, many in Basingstoke but also further afield with rail links to London and the M3 motorway affording easy opportunities for travel. In 2020 a telecommunication firm based on the outskirts of the village employed *c*.120 people, although few from the parish. A number of people worked from home and small businesses occupied converted farm buildings. The Queen Inn, two golf courses and a cricket centre provided other employment.

Farming

The Agricultural Landscape

BEFORE ENCLOSURE LARGE COMMONS (507 a.) provided pasture for sheep and other animals. Dummer Down, Priest Down and Cow Down lay on the higher chalklands, Dummer Down on the western border of the parish, Priest Down on the south-eastern side adjoining Nutley, and Cow Down probably south of Dummer Down, adjoining Popham.[1] Common fields, divided into narrow strips, were cultivated for crops including wheat, barley, oats, peas and vetches. Four arable fields (1,174 a.), Grange Field, Dummer Field, Breadless Field and Stoke Field, surrounded the village.[2] Paths and droves to the commons and between fields were important for access. Their width and maintenance were frequently the subject of orders in the manorial courts, as was the making and maintenance of hedges that divided fields and provided security on the parish boundaries. Woodland was limited; small areas of mixed deciduous trees included

1   HRO, 10M57/74–5. Cow Down is not marked on the enclosure map but is referred to in a list of roads and tracks: 'from south end of Dummer Down drove to Popham across Cow Down'.
2   HRO, 10M57/74–5. Breadless field, also known as Breadels.

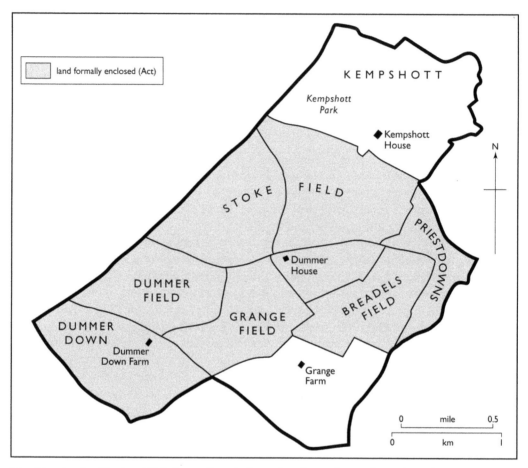

Map 4 *Land enclosed by Act of 1743; Grange Farm in the south and Kempshott in the north are shown as unaffected.*

Rowley Copse in the east with Helworthy Copse[3] and Stubbs Copse in the north of the parish. The 14th-century familial name 'de Stainford' suggests a stony brook, and a water course is mentioned in manorial court records of 1597.[4] However, with no significant surface streams or rivers, water for animals and crops depended on artificial ponds (including dew ponds) and wells bored into the chalk aquifer. The Grange was never subdivided and the land was worked as one farm. Lying south of the village and the high point of Tidley Hill (571 ft./174 m.), it contained two areas of woodland, Grange Copse and Bottom Copse.

The landscape changed markedly after 1743 with the enclosure of the common fields. Owners or right-holders of scattered arable strips were allocated blocks of land equating to their previous holdings with smaller, mostly rectangular fields created in Stoke Field and Grange Field for that purpose, divided by hedges, often hawthorn. The common downland pastures predominantly belonged to Michael Terry, lord of the manor, and remained an open 'prairie' landscape until later conversion to arable farming and

3   Variants: Healworth (1743), Kelworth (1864), Peat (1872) and Peak Copse (2019).
4   Gilbert de Stainford; HRO, 55M67/M4; below, Social History.

meadow, a pattern found across much of Hampshire.[5] A supply of water to the fields was first installed by Sir Richard Rycroft in 1898 and with improvements in 1926 reached most of the parish.[6] Prior to the installation of mains water in 1950, a reservoir at Grange farm fed from a deep bore held 20,000 gallons with a storage tank of 5,000 gallons.[7] The soil was described in that year as 'easy working, medium to heavy loam'.[8] Chalk pits scattered throughout the parish were a feature found across the Hampshire downs, chalk blocks employed as building material and burnt lime used as a soil improver.

Kempshott, in the period that it was included in the parish (1879–1989), consisted of parkland belonging to Kempshott House, two farms and more extensive woodland than found elsewhere in Dummer. By 2020 the agricultural landscape of Kempshott had been transformed by housing developments. Suburban housing estates had also spread from Basingstoke into parts of Dummer lying north of the M3 motorway. The larger part of the parish, south of the motorway, consisted of rolling farmland with well-hedged, tree-lined fields and small woodland clumps, little changed from the late 19th century.

Farming and Estate Management before 1536

In 1086 the two manors known later as East and West Dummer both consisted of five hides and each possessed five ploughlands, although only four were in cultivation in each manor. East Dummer had been worth 100s. in 1066 but was only 60s. in 1086, while a similar reduction was recorded in West Dummer, which fell from a value of 60s. to that of 40s. These smaller post-Domesday manors were held in demesne, East Dummer with two villagers and three smallholders and West Dummer with eight villagers, nine smallholders and three slaves. In East Dummer 1 a. of demesne meadow was recorded.[9] In 1341 the ninth of sheaves, fleeces and lambs was said to be 50s. and the parish claimed itself unable to meet the church taxation.[10] There is little other documentation for subsequent medieval agriculture at Dummer and impressions must therefore be built on other better documented manors in the area and from later Dummer evidence.[11] Farming would have been mixed, with a characteristic emphasis, as elsewhere in the chalklands, on sheep flocks. Beyond the arable common fields would have lain large areas of downland pasture.

The third manor, Dummer Grange, was developed by Waverley Abbey, a Cistercian house in Surrey during the 12th century. It was a farmstead whose lands lay outside the open fields, probably representing the colonisation of downland. The Grange was about 23 miles (37 km) distant and within a day's ride from the mother house. It would have been directly administered by the abbey and its reeve and was one of 15 granges

---

5   Chapman and Seeliger, *Enclosure in Hampshire*, xxiii.
6   HRO, 149A10/B17/1/1.
7   HRO, 5M70/27; above, Introduction.
8   HRO, 5M70/27.
9   *Domesday*, 108, 121.
10 *Nonarum Inquisitiones*, 121; below, Religious History.
11 For a neighbouring downland manor, albeit with a very different lord, see J. Hare, 'Hampshire Agriculture in the Middle Ages: the bishop of Winchester's manor of North Waltham', *Proc. Hants. F.C.* 75.1 (2020), 63–74, 75.

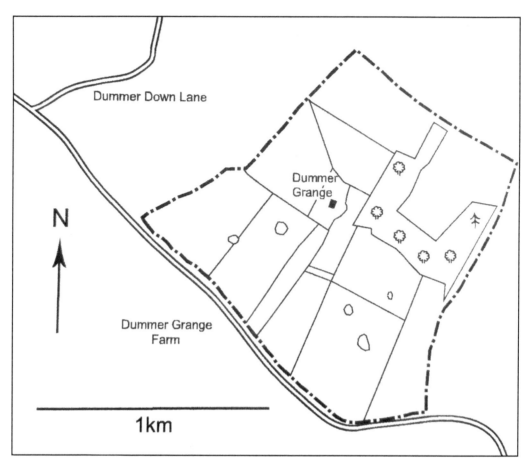

Map 5 *Waverley Abbey estates, Dummer boundary.*

belonging to the abbey, providing food or cash from the sale of grain, meat or wool.[12] The emergence of the Grange led to conflict between abbey and rector of Dummer over the tithes of grain produced, as in 1276.[13] Its value was given as 40*s.* in 1291, rising to 50*s.* by 1535.[14] By this time the Grange, as with other similar monastic properties, was leased to secular tenants, the rental value serving as the principal source of income for the abbey.[15]

Farming and Estate Management 1536–1743

Each manor had its own demesne farm – East and West Dummer and the Grange – although each may frequently have been leased. The Grange remained as a separate unit with a farmer and employed labourers. In East and West Dummer the traditional system

12   Service, *Waverley Abbey,* 223; above, Landownership.
13   HRO, 8M68/1; East Sussex Records Office, BAT 1496.
14   *Tax. Eccl.,* 215; *Valor Eccl.,* II, 35.
15   Service, *Waverley Abbey,* 223–4.

of farming continued with the demesne-owned land and that of tenants intermingled in the common fields and their animals pastured together on the commons. Sheep and corn husbandry, found in other downland manors in north Hampshire, was practised, with wheat and barley the main crops and sheep the chief livestock, providing wool for the local cloth industry as well as meat and manure.

Records of the manorial courts provide detailed information about farming practices in the 16th and 17th century.[16] The main purpose of the courts was to state and revise if necessary the customs of the manor relating to both land tenure and land use and to enforce payment of all monies and performance of services due to the lord. Details of land tenure – who held what, by what means and what dues and services were owed – were essential for the administration of the manor and from time to time were captured by a court of survey. One held for East Dummer in 1655 listed five freeholders, nine copyholders and two leaseholders.[17] Manorial lords routinely imposed entry payments when new tenants entered the manor and a heriot or best beast on the death of a tenant or surrender of a tenement. Thus in 1666, when William Vice sold a messuage and land, the new owner not only had to swear an oath of fealty to the lord but pay 6s. rent annually and a heriot of an ox or bull to the value of 30s., while in 1680 William Soper, a free tenant in West Dummer, having died, his son William inherited paying heriot of a cow valued at 25s.[18]

The court rolls reveal the continuation of a tightly ordered system of land use in which large common fields divided into narrow strips were cultivated by numerous individuals and a stint (ration of animals) established for grazing on the common fields and on the downland pastures beyond. Court proceedings show the need for co-operation between farmers and tenants both in growing their crops and in protecting the common pasture from outside animals or loss of their animals to another parish. Regulations – the customary practices of the manor – were restated at the start of each new lordship, and intervening courts issued requirements for particular seasons – reflecting weather conditions – and manorial officers, including haywards.[19] Supervisors of sheep or cattle were monitored and reported breaches of orders and fines were imposed by the courts on offenders. A bailiff worked for the lord of the manor(s), overseeing his interests.[20]

In 1537 the demesne farm of West Dummer had seven virgates (c.210 a.) of common arable land dispersed throughout the fields.[21] Other holdings varied in size: George Withers, yeoman (d. 1586) held 68 a.; Stephen Minchin, husbandman (d. 1588) held 11 a.[22] Withers grew 25 a. of wheat, 25 a. of barley and smaller amounts of oats, peas and vetches, valued at £45.[23] Minchin grew a similar mix of crops which were valued at £6 13s. 4d. Common field agriculture required the community to work together, and duties such as the making and maintenance of the hedges around the wheat field and the barley field were imposed by the courts. In 1560 the wheat field was to be sufficiently hedged by the Feast of the Nativity of the Virgin Mary (8 Sept.), with a fine of 10s. for

16   HRO, 55M67/3–37; below, Local Government.
17   HRO, 55M67/M29.
18   HRO, 65M72/PZ3.
19   Below, Local Government.
20   An example, HRO, 55M67/M13, '… for a Heriot one cow which the Bailiff took for the use of the Lord'.
21   HRO, 55M67/M30.
22   HRO, 1586A/89; 1588B/013.
23   HRO, 1586A/89.

non-compliance, but in 1598 the date was changed to St Leonard's Day (6 Nov.), perhaps reflecting changing seasons and planting practices.[24] References to the 'wheat field' and 'barley field' suggest a three-course rotation.[25] Once the crops were harvested, animals were let onto the stubbled fields. This too was tightly controlled: the lord's steward instructed the haywards on when this could happen and in what sequence. Horses were given priority; an ancient custom that only horses should be let in the stubble fields at the breach was replaced in 1583 by one that allowed a cow or calf to be substituted if a tenant had no horse, but only if he owned at least half a yardland.[26] Cattle and swine followed with fines for any who contravened these orders.

Large sheep flocks included the 470 sheep of Gilbert Withers (d. 1599), a yeoman who leased the demesne farm of East Dummer; the flock was valued at £130 and had been built up from the 124 sheep owned by his father, George. The Withers were a well-known Hampshire family.[27] John Grant (Graunt) (d. 1557) of the Grange, three generations of whose family farmed in the parish during the 16th century, had a flock of 320 sheep, while Henry Dummer (d. 1540), lord of West Dummer, left 120 sheep among his children.[28] Flocks were held not only by the three demesne farmers. The 34 wills and 29 inventories surviving from the 16th century show that most other testators kept sheep, the numbers varying from just two or three to the 120 owned by Thomas Morrell (d. 1554).[29] A middle-range smallholding was that of John Gold (d. 1599), husbandman, who had 30 sheep and 12 a. of crops along with two cows, four horses and a plough.[30]

Animals were pastured on the common downs. In 1560 the East Dummer court ordered that there were to be no more than eight sheep an acre with six cows and two horses or there could be more horses but fewer cows. John Wodeson who overpastured the common by just one animal was fined 6d., but a fine of 6s. 8d. could be imposed for more serious offences.[31] A court held in West Dummer in 1583 set the number of sheep on Dummer Down as a maximum of 300 with 30 beasts or horses. This was a reduction of 20 sheep from an order of 1564 to enable the horses to have sufficient feed when they came out of their stables.[32] Freeholders and copyholders were allowed 60 sheep and two beasts per yardland (30 a.) but cottagers were restricted to only ten sheep and two beasts.[33] Seasonal differences were recognised. In April 1597 a court for East and West Dummer ordered that with the consent of the freeholders and copyholders no cattle were to be pastured on Cow Down that year until the Feast of St Mark the Evangelist (25 Apr.) because 'Spring is backward by reason of the drith of the season'.[34]

24   HRO, 55M67/M19, 55M57/M25.
25   *VCH Oxon.* XVIII, *Brightwell Baldwin, Farms and Farming 1500–1800*, 103. Vetches were probably grown in the third year or the land was left fallow.
26   HRO, 55M67/M35.
27   HRO, 1599B/50; R.F. Bigg-Wither, *Materials for a History of the Wither Family* (Winchester, 1907); below, Social History.
28   HRO, 1557U/199; 1540B/26.
29   HRO, 1554B/069.
30   HRO, 1599AD/17.
31   HRO, 55M67/M19.
32   HRO, 55M67/M35.
33   HRO, 55M67/M35.
34   HRO, 55M67/M4; 'drith' refers to the drought, i.e., a dry, and presumably cold, winter: *Oxford English Dict.* 'dryth, n.' (accessed 20 Jan. 2022).

Sheep provided wool for the local cloth trade, so important in Basingstoke and its hinterland from the 15th century to the 17th, as well as meat and manure. While sheep were the main livestock, cattle, pigs and poultry were also important. Cattle were kept primarily as dairy animals providing milk for butter and cheese, not only meeting a family's requirements but also a marketable commodity in nearby Basingstoke. Numbers ranged from one or two cows per household to the 26 cows and bullocks owned by John Grant and Gilbert Withers respectively.[35] Evidence of cheese and butter making is found in several inventories, including that of the rector William White (d. 1588).[36] Ownership of swine was widespread; Gilbert Withers kept 38 hogs and pigs, probably the highest number in the parish, and had four flitches of bacon in his larder.[37] Withers also kept ten ducks, along with a cock and 19 hens, many others kept poultry, usually a cock and a number of hens. Horses appear to have been most often used for tractive power, unusual as oxen normally predominated in the 16th century. About 50 horses are recorded, sometimes designated as 'cart horses', but only one mention is made of oxen.[38] The 16 horses recorded at East Manor Farm with 'all harness and furniture' and also two saddles suggest that most were used with the three ploughs and carts but that two were reserved for riding.[39]

Extant probate material from the 17th century, which consists of 40 wills and 41 inventories, the latter totalling £4,060 and ranging from £5 to £690, reveals those with limited means as well as some very prosperous yeomen. Sheep flocks of 450 owned by Richard Penton (d. 1688) and 270 held by Walter Madgwick (d. 1626) equalled those of the previous century. Madgwick had both freehold and copyhold land in the parish and his inventory, valued at £211, included 28 cattle. At the Grange, William Soper, gentleman (d. 1688), and his widow Amy (d. 1700) had a flock of 250 sheep and with cattle and swine the total value of their livestock amounted to £138. Their crops, which included 35 a. of wheat, 26 a. of peas, oats and barley in the barn, were valued at £100. The 14 sides of bacon and beef in the cellar along with eight (beer) barrels indicate a comfortable standard of living. On a more modest scale, George Ilsley (d. 1668), yeoman kept 80 sheep, two horses, 11 beasts, nine hogs and pigs, which, with corn and his plough, cart and two harrows, was valued at £117. It was not until 1655 that every poor man was allowed to keep one hog or pig, rescinding a requirement for arable land ownership.[40] An interesting combination of activities is shown by a weaver, Ralph Curtis (d. 1612), who had 16 stalls of bees sufficient to supply wax for candles and honey for the village and perhaps to be sold more widely.

The manorial courts remained active in protecting common land in the 17th century. In 1604 Walter Madgwick encroached on waste or common land at Staples in Cow Lane by erecting his own ditch there and digging beyond what was allowed. Five men were appointed to see that he reinstated the land and restored the water course.[41] In 1615 orders were made, doubtless reflecting earlier ones, for 'no hedge [to] be removed until thought good or convenient without general consent' and for 'no man [to] carry away

35   HRO, 1588A/030; 1557U/119; 1599B/50.
36   HRO, 1588B/73.
37   HRO, 1599B/50.
38   HRO, 1561U/22; 1558U/054.
39   HRO, 1599B/50.
40   HRO, 55M67/M11; M29.
41   HRO, 55M67/M4.

any other man's hedge or fence'.[42] There was to be 'no gleaning of corn on any other man's land by self, children or servants' and 'no weeding other than in own corn'. Verges were to be kept around fields, crops were not to be sown out to the hedges, traditional harvest ways were to be maintained and the width of the Drove was to be kept at 14 yds between Stubbs Copse and Grove Gate, presumably to enable the use of large carts and wagons.[43] Care was taken to preserve the grazing quality of the commons and the court orders of 1623 reflect others made throughout the period – cattle had to be taken off Dummer Down by the day before All Saints' (31 Oct.); the downs were then to be laid afresh at Candlemas (2 Feb.) and broken (animals allowed back in) on Hockmonday.[44]

The reason why this traditional way of farming, and, indeed, way of life, ended is indicated in a lease of 1723 concerning land belonging to a yeoman, Richard Poynter:

> Eight and a half acres arable dispersed in common field (i.e. one and a half acres in Bridles Field on Sturrum Hill; one and a half acres in Bridles Field beside footway from Dummer to Nutley; one acre in Grange Field at Paine Stile; one and half acres in Dummer Field crossing the Milkway from Dummer to the Cow Down; one acre in Dummer Field at place called Hendon; one acre in Stoke Field at Thorn Dell; one acre in same near Bunting Dell with all commons, ways, etc.)[45]

The difficulties in cultivating such scattered holdings and the advantages of being able to implement new agricultural techniques in consolidated fields led the lord of the manor and others to seek an Act of Parliament for enclosure of the common fields and of all common land within the parish.

Farming 1743–1926

Parliamentary enclosure with outside arbitrators was often preferred to informal enclosure when numerous owners, rights and interests were involved and enabled objective and legally binding decisions to be made on the best division of the land.[46] How agreement to this course of action was gained and whether there was opposition from those who lost use of the common wastes and gleaning rights is not known in the case of Dummer. The system favoured the larger landowners and seven small landowners refused to consent to the bill but as they did not appear at the parliamentary committee hearing, the Act was passed.[47]

Enclosure of the common lands in Dummer (1,174 a. open fields and 587 a. commons) was carried out by an Act of Parliament in 1743 promoted by Michael Terry (d. 1755), lord of the manor, Thomas Stockwell, rector, and other owners and proprietors

---

42   HRO, 55M67/M11.
43   HRO, 55M67/M3.
44   HRO, 55M67/M37. Hocktide was a movable feast, as it referred to the week following Easter.
45   HRO, 55M67/T81. Poynter was awarded 43 a. in the Enclosure Act of 1743. He presumably had other rights or lands.
46   Chapman and Seeliger, *Enclosure in Hampshire*, xiv–xxiv.
47   16 George II, 10 Jan., 11 Feb. 1742.

of land in the parish.[48] This was early for an enclosure act; neighbouring parishes of Basingstoke and Mapledurwell followed but not until 1788 and 1797 respectively.[49]

A map or plan prepared by Robert Scullard shows the new fields or blocks of land agreed by the specially appointed commissioners superimposed upon the earlier boundaries. Michael Terry was awarded 1,101 a., and 16 other owners, or those with rights, were granted 688 a. of land between them.[50] Twelve of these other landholders were yeomen and one the widow of a yeoman; probate material shows several of them to have had substantial means.[51] Field boundaries were set, many of which remain in the 21st century. These divisions formed the basis of later farms, examples including land in Stoke Field allocated to William Smith which became known as Little Manor Farm and Richard Soper's allocation of the larger half of Dummer Field becoming Soper's Farm.[52]

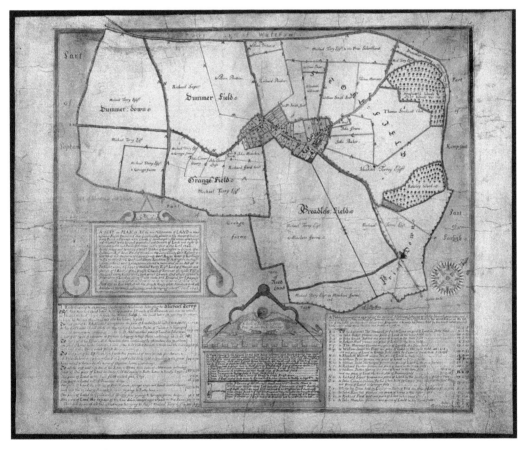

Map 6 *Dummer enclosure map, 1743.*

48   HRO, 55M67/E3.
49   HRO, Q23/2/7, and 1 and 2 maps and award; *Mapledurwell*, 35; J. Chapman and S. Seeliger, *Enclosure Environment and Landscape in Southern England* (Stroud, 2001), 37.
50   There is an unexplained difference of 28 a. between 1,789 a. common land and 1,761 a. of land awarded.
51   HRO, 1746B/003; 1749A/084; 1760B/39.
52   HRO, 12M49/A20/71.

The commons remained predominantly in the ownership of Michael Terry, who already possessed the East and West manors and the Grange, although an area of Dummer Down was attached to Grange Farm and an area of Priest Down was attached to Minchin's Farm.[53] A major beneficiary of enclosure was the rector, Thomas Stockwell, whose award of just over 78 a. of land in Stoke Field replaced an extraordinary 50 pieces of glebe land scattered across the parish, as well as his rights to cow and sheep commons.[54] The allocation allowed the creation of Glebe Farm.[55]

By the beginning of the 19th century the consolidation of land appears to have led to the desired effect of expanded arable farming outputs, with crop returns of 1801 showing 305 a. of wheat, 290 a. of barley, 250 a. of oats, 90 a. of turnips or rape, 60 a. of peas and 10 a. of potatoes.[56] In 1820 the Grange was 80 per cent arable, tithe free because the land had formerly belonged to Waverley Abbey. In 1840, 1,613 a. of the 1,770 a. land subject to tithes were estimated to be under arable cultivation.[57] This included 359 a. of wheat valued at £2,511, 240 a. of barley at £1,152 and 120 a. of oats at £660 as well as 519 a. of fodder crops, including sainfoin, turnips and vetches, valued at £958.[58]

A drive to improve standards of husbandry was evident when tenancies were agreed; a lease of Little Manor Farm in 1842 required the tenant to 'cultivate, crop, till, manure and manage the farm lands in a fair, proper and careful manner and not take two successive crops of wheat or other grain unless the same is followed with a summer fallow of at least three ploughings or a green crop (clover, peas, beans)'. If hay or straw was sold off the farm then one wagon of good rotten horse dung of 12s. value plus £3 was to be paid for every ton of straw sold, with a penalty of £2.[59] From 1866 turnips and swedes were increasingly used as fodder crops.[60] Rape cultivation increased from 10 a. in 1875 to 88 a. in 1921.[61]

Further consolidation took place during the century as opportunities were taken to purchase plots as they became available through the death of previous owners. Thomas Terry (d. 1829), lord of the manor, purchased about 15 a. of land in 1820 that had belonged to Thomas Baker in Stoke field and nearly 3 a. of land that had belonged to John Savage.[62] By 1835 Soper's farm had been joined with Dummer Down farm, and following the fire at Little Manor farmhouse in 1877 the farm buildings and arable land in Stoke field were sold to Sir Nelson Rycroft and added to the estate land farmed in hand.[63]

Sheep farming on the downlands continued. The Drivers in their report on Hampshire agriculture show Dummer with substantial flocks of 1,200 sheep.[64] The Terrys were at the head of the shift to Southdown sheep. In 1801 Thomas Terry bought 300 ewes from Lewes (Suss.), together with shorthorn rams to cross with his Hampshire ewes. Although initially ridiculed, the change was rapidly accepted and the Southdown

---

53   HRO, 10M57/A7/1–2.
54   HRO, 10M54/A7; 21M65/E15/32; below, Religious History.
55   Below, Religious History.
56   TNA, HO 67/24.
57   Service, *Waverley Abbey*, 241; HRO, 34M95/3. The total acreage of the parish was 2,081 a.
58   TNA, IR 18/8966.
59   HRO, 55M67/T55.
60   TNA, MAF 68/27.
61   TNA, MAF 68/413; 68/3026.
62   HRO, 55M67/T110.
63   HRO, 12M49/A20/7; 55M67/T58.
64   A. and W. Driver, *General View of the Agriculture of the County of Hants.* (London, 1794), 23–5.

became the dominant chalkland stock.[65] Together with this new breed came the cultivation of swedes, which allowed the maintenance of larger flocks during the winter. The Southdowns produced more lambs and were fatter, with improved carcasses and more wool.[66] Stephen Terry, lord of the manor and diarist, recorded 240 lambs 'doing well' in January 1842 and some fine Southdown wethers, a dual-purpose breed (meat and wool), feeding on turnips, hay, barley and chaff in November of the same year.[67] A sale of a breeding flock of Hampshire Downs at Dummer Down farm in July 1857 included 520 ewes and ewe lambs, and 29 rams and ram lambs. The flock was described as 'well-selected and highly esteemed' and must have been built up over a good number of years.[68] Numbers of sheep in the parish were 2,337 in 1866 but had nearly halved to 1,146 by 1875 and fell further to 924 in 1880 during the prolonged agricultural depression that started in the 1870s.[69] This was a picture that was replicated in neighbouring parishes which also depended on arable-based mixed farming systems as farmers competed with cheap imports of wheat and wool. A steep rise to 2,608 in 1890, a level which was sustained until at least 1911, can be partially explained by a shift to meat production – a movement widespread on chalklands during the depression in arable farming from the 1870s – and by the inclusion of Kempshott's figures, then part of the parish.[70]

Cattle were also important, and while dairy farming predominated, dual-purpose breeds such as the 18 shorthorn Durham cows mentioned by Stephen Terry in 1842 show that beef production was also undertaken. Dairy cows numbered 30 in 1866 with 21 other cattle which may refer to calves, bulls or beef cattle; there were 55 milkers and 49 others in 1890, 45 milkers and 157 others in 1901 and 37 milkers and 96 others in 1920.[71] Pig numbers grew from 65 in 1875 to 218 in 1890 but were half that number by 1911 and continued to decline thereafter.[72] The use of horses in agriculture is illustrated by Terry, who noted '2nd September: The last full load of oats came in from Windmill, 13 horses employed in carrying the oats to the home rickyard'; he also recorded five teams of horses stoning for turnips in Dell field. The highest number of horses in the parish was 87 in 1880, with 55 still in use in 1921. In the latter year poultry numbered over 1,000 fowls.[73]

Land use varied considerably, particularly the area given to pasture or permanent grass. In 1872 there were 94 a. of pasture and 1,904 a. of arable land, while in 1905 there was said to be 654 a. of permanent grass, largely Kempshott parkland in the north of the parish and 2,131 a. of land cultivated for crops including wheat, barley, oats and turnips.[74] This is partly explained by the number of sheep and cattle, both of which rose after 1870 leading to changes in land use, and partly by the inclusion of Kempshott in the parish from 1879.

65   E.L. Jones, 'Eighteenth-Century Changes in Hampshire Chalkland Farming,' *Agricultural History Rev.* viii (1960), 16.
66   Ibid., 17.
67   HRO, 24M49/1.
68   *Hants. Chron.*, 11 Jul. 1857.
69   TNA, MAF 68/27; 68/413; 68/698.
70   TNA, MAF 68/1268; 68/2465.
71   TNA, MAF 68/27; 68/1325; 68/1895; 68/3026. See above, water supply.
72   TNA, MAF 68/413; 68/1268; 68/2465.
73   HRO, 24M49/1.
74   OS 1st edn, 1:25000, sheets XXVI.1, 2, 5, 6, 9, and 10, 1872, *area book*; VCH Hants. III, 357.

Farming after 1926

The sale of the Kempshott and Dummer estate in 1926 followed the death of Sir Richard Rycroft, lord of the manor, marked a turning point in farming and in parish life as a whole.[75] Nine farms, many cottages and 2,150 a. of land were sold.[76] A previous agent was reported as saying that Rycroft had kept a large area of land in hand and while at one time it had made a good return, for several years past it had lost heavily, adding that generally speaking it was poor farming country.[77] A number of farmhouses were sold away from the land and with some new landowners now living outside the parish, farm managers or farm companies were appointed with responsibility for one or more farms.[78] The farms sold were Manor, Little Manor, Glebe, Clump, Tower Hill, Village, Southwood, Kennel and Kempshott. The last was partially a market garden holding with 2 a. of walled kitchen garden, two vineries, a tomato house, soft fruit and orchards. Southwood and Kennel farms were tenanted. Kennel was a mixed farm of 153 a. Southwood had land in Deane and Wootton St Lawrence parishes as well as Dummer with Kempshott. The farmhouse, 48 a. arable and 28 a. pasture and over 3 a. of woodland were in the parish.

Figure 19 *Manor Farm House in 1926.*

75   Above, Landownership.
76   HRO, 10M57/SP375; 149A10/B17/1.
77   HRO, 174A12/A2, 102.
78   As an example, Heathfield Growers farmed Grange, Manor, Clump, Glebe and Dummer Down Farms in 1941: TNA, 32/974/64. In 1981 there were seven farmers and three managers.

Manor Farm with 307 a. of land was the main agricultural holding sold, described as a 'valuable dairy and corn farm' with an 'excellent set of farm buildings'. Apart from 22 a. of land and two cottages, all the land was held in hand, divided between pasture and arable. The buildings were separated by a concrete road with a barn, timber store, stabling for six cart horses, loose boxes and a cowshed for 12 on one side; on the other side 'modern buildings' included a dairy and cooling room, cow stalls for 16 and a detached cow house for six, a bull box and yard, a cow house for four and a range of ten piggeries. At Village Farm, also dairy and corn, 177 a. were sold; at Clump Farm 187 a. of pasture and arable land were sold, as was the meadow land behind Little Manor farmhouse and the meadow land of Glebe Farm. Tower Hill, described as a mixed farm of 87 a. with a large two-bay barn, granary and other farm buildings, completed the sale.

During the Second World War arable farming necessarily took precedence over livestock but actual numbers of animals in the parish were quite high. In 1941 the group of farms – Manor, Clump and Glebe – had 122 sheep and 22 cattle, Grange Farm had 102 sheep and 70 cattle, Kennel Farm had 91 sheep and Southwood Farm had over 70 each of sheep and cattle.[79] By 1951 there were no sheep in the parish but they were re-introduced, with 800 in 1961 and nearly 600 in 1981, before economic conditions saw their eventual demise.[80] In 2020 the only sheep in the parish were a small flock kept to maintain an 8 a. field close to Dummer House and 25 sheep at Dummer Down Farm, also kept for land maintenance and for sustainable meat.[81] Cattle numbers increased steadily after the war, rising to 1,559 in 1981. The Dummanor herd of pedigree Holstein Friesians established in 1948 by Colonel Andrew Ferguson (d. 1966) was sold in March 1991.[82] In 1950 a pedigree Ayrshire herd formed part of a sale of Dummer Grange.[83] A beef herd was added and fattened over 18 months, giving a break to the arable fields.[84] The dairy operation at Manor Farm, owned by Colonel Clifton (d. 1996), ceased in the late 1970s/ early 1980s after two episodes of brucellosis.[85] In 2020 a small herd of Longhorn cows was kept by a 'hobby' farmer.[86]

Pig numbers also rose after the war, reaching 317 in 1961.[87] Peter Chase took over Southwood Farm from Sir David Beale in 1968 and his venture of 240 sows for weaner production was still operating in 1986.[88] The total number of pigs in the parish by the early 1980s was over 1,200. Twelve horses were still in agricultural use in 1951. Poultry, important from 1920 to the 1960s, peaked in 1951 with 2,267 fowls.[89] Village Farm kept nearly 1,000 fowls in 1941 but struggled during the war to obtain feed and were reduced to using baker's sweepings.[90] Turkey farming, recorded in 1961 (361 birds), appears to have been a short-lived venture.

79   TNA, MAF 32/974/64.
80   TNA, MAF 68/4349; 68/4724; 68/5750.
81   Barry Dodd and Andrew Ferguson. pers. comms 2019.
82   http://thepeerage.com/p10146.htm (accessed 23 Jul. 2019).
83   HRO, 5M70/27.
84   Charles Palmer-Tomkinson, pers. comm., 2019.
85   Ibid.
86   Pers. obs., June 2019.
87   TNA, MAF 68/4724.
88   *Scats Sentinel*, July/Aug. 1988, 2.
89   TNA, MAF 68/5750.
90   TNA, MAF 32/974/64; HRO, 51M76/H/2B1.

The amount of land under crops varied throughout this period. At the Grange in 1950 ley farming was practised with 130 a. grass of a total 346 a. and water laid on to every field. Crops included wheat, barley and oats.[91] Wheat crops in the parish ranged from 271 a. in 1941 to 841 a. in 1981, barley from 549 a. to 778 a., while the quantity of oats grown dropped from 391 a. to 31 a. in the same period. Turnips (74 a.), used for fodder in 1941, had almost disappeared by the 1970s–80s. Cabbage, kale and rape were important crops during the Second World War, with mustard introduced after the war; 222 a. of mustard were produced in 1951.[92]

The Hutton family of Mapledurwell made Dummer the base of their farming activities from 1948, first at Oakdown and then also at Village Farm.[93] In 2020 Alan Hutton farmed a number of fields between the village and the A30, other land having been developed for housing.[94] Major Archie Coats (d. 1989) bought Tower Hill farmhouse and surrounding land in 1953, becoming one of only a few professional pigeon shooters in the country, known for his Ten Acre Shoots held twice a year until the 1980s. He was also a member of the Rabbit Clearance Society, pest control being one of his great preoccupations. His books, *The Amateur Keeper: A Handbook for the Small Shoot* (1962) and *Pigeon Shooting* (1963), remain standard texts.[95] In 1953, the Ferguson family moved to Dummer Down Farm and ran a large dairy farm until 1991 when they diversified, letting redundant farm buildings to small businesses, with a limited acreage of land farmed by a contractor.

Farming in 2020 was largely arable, the main crops being wheat and barley, with an exception at Kennel Farm, where an equestrian business was run on a small area of land adjacent to the farmhouse, the M3 motorway having divided and destroyed the viability of the holding. A number of farms in the area had come together in 2003 to form the Wheatsheaf Farming Company, a single arable business aiming to increase the soil's ability to look after itself and reduce the need for chemical and mechanical intervention. Dummer Down, Dummer Grange and Southwood farms were initial participants, with Folly Farm in North Waltham. A practice of minimum tillage and break crops, such as beans, rape and linseed, was altered in 2015 to one of zero tillage and cover crops, a mixture of six to eight species including clover and vetches – the roots providing essential nutrients.[96] Dummer Grange, also farming Manor and Clump farmland and known as Grange Manor Farms, and Folly Farm remained part of the group in 2020.[97]

Woodland

No woodland was recorded in the Domesday survey, but it is likely that some existed and was carefully managed during the Middle Ages. The management and use of the common woods and coppices was carefully regulated later. A pattern of coppicing each year for seven years was practised in the woods then left for a year to recover. In 1623

91   HRO, 5M70/27.
92   TNA, MAF 68/3979; 68/4349; 68/5224; 68/5750.
93   *Mapledurwell*, 40.; *P.O. Dir. Hants.* 1955, 185–6; 1958, 201–2.
94   Barry Dodd, pers. comm., 2019.
95   HRO, 64M99/B255/10.
96   www.britishfarmingawards.co.uk/david-miller (accessed 18 Sept. 2019).
97   *Design Statement*, in 2002 amalgamation of three major arable farms in the parish.

tenants were ordered to depasture and feed their cattle in Rowley, Helworthy and Stubbs copses from the time of seven years' growth until coppiced.[98] In 1666 the common woods were to be laid open at seven years' growth for that year.[99] Oak trees received special attention as property of the lord. Oak was needed to provide suitable wood for house building and as a cash crop. These trees do not grow well on chalk soil, which is more suited to those with shallow roots, but there were oak trees in the parish and in 1615 it was ordered that no one was to cut any oak or sprig of oak likely to become a tree on the waste common unless between Christmas and Candlemas (2 Feb.) under threat of a fine of 10s.[100] As late as 1729 tenants were forbidden from cutting oak rods or bushes within 1 a. breadth of the common hedges by the manor's ways and were to protect oak trees in their own hedges, with fines of 6s. 8d. for any offences.[101]

Although woodland was limited – 95 a. in 1837 when it was stated that one tenth of the wood was cut annually – regular sales of underwood and prime wood took place between 1829 and 1868 at Helworthy, Stubbs, Bottom and Fuller's copses. In 1850 William Tubb sold 50 oak and 22 ash trees in Grange Copse.[102] In 1870 woodland had increased to 149 a.[103] The highest acreage of woodland recorded was 268 a. in 1905, when Kempshott, more heavily wooded, was included.[104]

In 1950, 35 a. of woodland and a newly planted larch plantation of 4–5 a. were recorded at Dummer Grange.[105] A new mixed plantation, Sunset Wood (8 a.), was planted north-west of Dummer Down Lane in the late 20th century by Geoffrey and Fiona Squire.[106]

Agricultural Employment

The gradual retreat from owner or lessee occupation to landless wage labour post-enclosure can be seen across the 19th and 20th centuries. A comparison of occupations between 1851 and 1901 shows that agricultural jobs were predominant. In 1851, of a population of 409, there were five farmers, and a bailiff with over 50 agricultural labourers, including two shepherds. All the farms had resident farm servants, young men aged between 15 and 23, hired on an annual basis, suggesting that the system of servants in husbandry survived at this date.[107] Fifty years later, in 1901, with a population of 390, there was one farmer, two farm bailiffs, a farm steward and about 70 men and boys employed in a variety of agricultural work including six shepherds, two cattlemen and a game keeper. No servants in husbandry remained.[108] The 1911 census shows an increase in cowmen to six and an assistant, a dairyman and assistant, a new occupation of traction

98   HRO, 55M67/M37.
99   HRO, 55M67/M15.
100 As an example, HRO, 55M67/M11.
101 HRO, 55M67/M3.
102 *Hants. Chron.*, 26 Oct. 1829; 27 Oct. 1834; 19 Oct. 1850; 17 Oct. 1868.
103 TNA, MAF 68/242.
104 *VCH Hants.* III, 357.
105 HRO, 5M70/27.
106 Barry Dodd, pers. comm., 2019.
107 A. Kussmaul, *Servants in Husbandry in Early Modern England* (Cambridge, 1981), Ch. 7, 120–34.
108 *Census*, 1851, 1901. The 1851 census included Winslade with Kempshott, inflating these figures. The 1901 figures relate to the civil parish of Dummer with Kempshott.

engine driver and a few men acting as hedgers and thatchers as well as farm labourers. An unusual occupation was that of truffler, recorded in 1861.

A picture of the intensity of manpower involved in agricultural work is given by Stephen Terry, who in 1841 recorded 32 people cutting and tying 'magnificent' white oats and later that year described 63 people enjoying the harvest supper. His comments on 'thankfulness for the crops in such hard times' is a reminder of the economic hardships faced by agricultural workers and of the conditions which had led to the Swing Riots of 1830.[109] Wages of 9s. a week in 1795 had risen only marginally after the riots and attempts to prevent the introduction of threshing machines – seen as a threat to jobs – had been unsuccessful. Terry records, '14 August, 1842: Barber's threshing machine at work and on our wheat'. Workers came together in forming branches of two Friendly Societies to help support themselves and their families, and this help continued to be needed, especially during the agricultural depression of the 1870s. The invitation to Joseph Arch, president of the National Agricultural Labourers' Union, to address a meeting in the Primitive Methodist chapel in Dummer in 1882 signifies the level of their concern at this time.[110]

The number of people engaged in agriculture varied from 78 in 1921 to just 39 in 1941 before rising after the Second World War to reach 76 in 1981, almost the same level as 60 years earlier. Considering the introduction of machinery, this was an unusually high figure at this date, probably explained by an increase in horticulture from 12 a. in 1971 to 87 a. in 1981.[111] Market gardening was undertaken on land which later became used as Dummer golf course. Throughout the 1970s crops included a yearly average of 46 a. of Brussels sprouts and 10–15 a. of cabbage; workers packed sprouts on site which were supplied to a major supermarket.[112] Pig and poultry farming were also labour-intensive enterprises. By 2001 only 13 people worked on the land, and this fell to nine people involved in agriculture in 2011.[113]

Industry, Crafts, Commerce and Services

The Cloth Industry

By the 15th and early 16th century the Basingstoke area had a flourishing cloth industry which depended on wool from flocks of sheep pastured on the surrounding chalk downlands.[114] Basingstoke merchants helped supply the demands for textiles in England and Europe, selling wool and cloth often spun and woven in the nearby villages. Dummer formed part of this wider industrial hinterland. The earliest records are those of William Reading (d. 1555), whose inventory included looms and weaving equipment, and that of a weaver, Robert Weston, who died in the same year and whose inventory included a loom and three yards of kersey (a standard, mid-grade cloth named after

109 HRO, 24M49/1; below, Social History.
110 *Hants. Chron.*, 7 Oct. 1882; *ODNB*, s.v. Arch Joseph (1826–1919), Trade Unionist and Politician (accessed 9 Jul. 2018); below, Social History.
111 *Census*, 1921–81.
112 Barry Dodd, pers. comm., 2019, Major Ronald Ferguson's undertaking 1971–9.
113 www.nomisweb.co.uk/reports/localarea?compare=E0400448 (accessed 7 Sept. 2019).
114 J. Hare, *Basingstoke: A Medieval Town, c.1000–c.1600* (London, 2017), 30–7.

Kersey, Suff.).[115] Both families continued as spinners.[116] Two wills of the Madgwick family indicate how the industry affected the village. Nicholas Madgwick (d. 1566) a clothier, possessed wool, making bequests of 70 tods of 'good fleece wool' and cloth. Spinners infrequently appear in the wills and inventories, as before mechanisation it was a domestic trade with low capital requirements, but Nicholas left money to groups of spinners in Dummer, nearby Northington and elsewhere.[117] His son Nicholas (d. 1577) lived at Dummer but had a workshop in Overton – a small town and local centre for the cloth trade to the west of Basingstoke – with three looms and a range of cloth including 19 white kerseys worth £50.[118] In the early 17th century Ralph Curtis, a weaver (d. 1612), whose inventory which was valued at £55, included a loom and implements for weaving in his shop as well as 90 sheep.[119] Other testators possessed quantities of wool but the last record is that of 1668, from when it would appear that the great cloth production years had passed.[120]

Milling

With no rivers in the parish, farmers relied on windmills for processing their grain. There were two windmills in Dummer; one featured in the 1743 enclosure awards[121] and in 1838 was described as a post mill with four common sails, situated on the highest point in the parish at Priest Down, Dummer Clump, near the border with Farleigh parish.[122] The date of its construction and demise are unknown.

The other mill was a smock mill belonging to Little Manor farm occupied by the Smith family for several generations who described themselves as yeomen. It was built in 1811 by Mr Day of Westerham (Kent)[123] when James Smith senior assigned the lease of the farm to his son James and John Banister of Eversley, yeoman 'with the addition of a windmill erected thereon'.[124] As well as the Smith family, mortgage records from 1810 to 1827 variously show shared interest in the mill from John Kidgell of East Oakley, John Webb of Quidhampton (Wilts.) and Nathaniel Loader of Basingstoke. The mortgage in 1810 for the farm was £500 but by 1827 had increased to £2,300 indicating that the farm and mill was a successful business with shareholders prepared to risk investment.[125] John Thorp, a farmer in Preston Candover, noted a payment to Mr Smith in 1818 for grinding two sacks of barley at a cost of 4s.,[126] suggesting that the mill served a wider area than just the village.

115 HRO, 1555B/58; 1555B/81.
116 HRO, 1574B/140; 1564B/105.
117 TNA, PROB 11/48/417.
118 HRO, 1577AD/27.
119 HRO, 1612AD/029.
120 HRO, 1609A/33; 1612A/63; 1621B/50; 1627A/31; 1631AD/70; 1668A/067.
121 HRO, 120M97/1; HRO, 10M57/A7/1–2; NGR SU 603459; Mills Archive Trust, 26289, K. Kirsopp, *Notebook of Hampshire Windmills Alton-Froxfield*.
122 HRO, 10M57/A7/1–2.
123 *Hants. Chron.*, 11 Aug. 1828; Mills Archive Trust, 26289, Kirsopp, *Notebook of Hampshire Windmills Alton-Froxfield*; NGR approx. SU 58574712.
124 HRO, 55M67/T40, 55M67/T41.
125 HRO, 55M67/T39–45.
126 HRO, 66M82/3.

Revd Arthur Atherley Hammond of Southampton leased Little Manor farm for
14 years to William Drinkwater, yeoman of Dummer, in 1830 at a rent of £120 per
annum.[127] The milling equipment, valued at £55, included two pairs of 4 ft French stones
for milling wheat and two worn-out millstone grit stones for barley complete with flour
and grist machines and bolting mill.[128] The newspaper advertisement said that the village
had the advantage of a mealman and that the next nearest mill was six miles away. The
Basingstoke canal was within easy distance for conveyance of goods to London in 24
hours.[129] The last miller in the Smith family, another James, died intestate in December
1831 leaving administration of his goods valued at £450.[130] There are no records of who
took over the mill after James's death.

Disaster struck during the night of 31 May 1833 when a traveller on the turnpike
road noticed the mill was on fire.[131] Flour dust mixed with air is very flammable and
mill fires were common. The newspaper reported that as the mill had not been worked
for the previous three weeks it was assumed that it had been the victim of an arson
attack following another in the village a few weeks previously.[132] The mill was not rebuilt
but millwrights William Hosier and William Flowers still lived in the village in 1839
and 1841 respectively.[133] The next nearest mills were in Basingstoke and Sherborne St
John, which lay at some distance away.[134] There was little evidence of either mill in the
landscape in 2020 apart from a field named Millfield.

Smiths and Other Crafts

A blacksmith worked in the village in 1638 when Richard Willmott's anvil, vices, scales,
hammers and other equipment were valued at £5 13s. 4d.[135] He appointed Robert Warner
(d. 1640), another blacksmith, as one of his overseers.[136] No equipment was listed in
Warner's inventory, suggesting that he may have worked with Willmott rather than
running his own business. John Hare the elder leased his smith's shop called Monks in
1767;[137] one occupant was John Hall, blacksmith (d. 1774).[138] Richard Geary (d. 1761)
was also a blacksmith.[139] Monks had ceased to be a smithy by 1812.[140] In 1841 there were
five blacksmiths, three founders and a founder apprentice.[141] The Holland family became
foremost in the trade. John Holland (d. 1828)[142] passed the business on to his grandson

---

127 HRO, 55M67/T50.
128 HRO, 55M67/T52.
129 *Hants. Chron.*, 11 Aug. 1828; HRO, 55M67/T52.
130 HRO, 1832AD/56.
131 *Hants. Ad.*, 1 June 1833; *The Times*, 5 June 1833.
132 *The Times*, 5 June 1833.
133 HRO, baptism records; *Census*, 1841.
134 *The Times*, 5 June 1833; *Hants. Ad.*, 1 June 1833; *Hants. Chron.*, 3 June 1833.
135 HRO, 1638A/197.
136 HRO, 1640B/54.
137 HRO, 55M67/T70.
138 TNA, PROB 11/997/123.
139 *Public Ledger and Daily Advertiser*, 31 Dec. 1761.
140 HRO, 55M67/T70.
141 *Census*, 1841.
142 HRO, 1828A/45.

Figure 20 *Left: George Page outside Foundry House. Right: George making horseshoes with Jim Wilmot and Bert Stephens, c.1892.*

Henry Holland when he died in 1846.[143] His large foundry opposite the village school in Up Street[144] was put up for sale having a 139 ft. (42 m.) frontage to the street, yard with roomy workshops, shed and paddock. The sales particulars stated that the business had been carried on for many years conducting an extensive trade and was gradually improving in a respectable neighbourhood.[145] Censuses listed other blacksmiths, founders and moulders clustered around the property but James Allen (d. 1878) continued the business for at least the next two decades, employing five men including his stepsons James and William Holland as apprentices.[146] His wife Hannah described herself as a blacksmith in 1885, an unusual occupation for a woman.[147] James Allen, whitesmith worked in Dummer between 1834 and 1841.[148]

The trade in the village was sufficient to still support four blacksmiths in 1901 as well as George Page (d. 1927), iron founder at the Victoria Foundry in Up Street established in 1772.[149] He described himself as a shoeing and general smith, undertaker, wheelwright and carpenter. The smithy continued under successive owners and was still operating in 1939 when Reginald Page was the master blacksmith.[150] The Victoria Foundry was demolished *c.*1963 and two dwellings erected on the site.[151] James Wilmot ran a separate smithy at Tower Hill in 1881 to at least 1911.[152] With the decline in horsepower required

143 HRO, 1846AD/29.
144 *Census* 1891; OS 1:25,000 XXVI.6.
145 HRO, 10M57/C95.
146 *Census,* 1851, 1861, 1871.
147 *P.O. Dir. Hants.* 1885, 651.
148 HRO, 65M72.
149 *Census,* 1901; Willis Museum, Dummer folder.
150 *1939 Register.*
151 *Hants. and Berks. Gaz.,* 1960.
152 *Census,* 1881, 1891, 1911; *1939 Register.*

on farms, presumably the business soon closed after the Second World War. Another essential trade for agriculture was the wheelwright; the earliest recorded was Richard Bignell in 1803.[153] Three were mentioned from 1822 to 1830, with the Bignell family running a shop and sawhouse through two generations.[154] Two apprentices were taken on by two wheelwrights in the 1841 census but only one entry appeared in 1851 and 1861 and two in 1901.[155]

Occupations in the timber trade were well represented from 1815 to 1939 with carpenters, sawyers, cabinet makers and joiners. Some carpenters worked independently while others were employed on the large estates.[156] Hurdle makers and a sheep cage maker were employed in the mid 19th century when sheep farming was dominant.[157] Hurdles and windbreaks were still being made in the 1930s as well as rods, which were shipped to Staffordshire for the manufacture of crates for packing pottery.[158] As the village grew, building trades such as bricklayers, plumbers and plasterers developed alongside the carpenters, peaking in numbers in 1881. Considering the number of 18th- and 19th-century thatched houses in the village, there were very few thatchers listed, with just one in 1851 and two in 1911.[159]

The Billimore family ran a boot and shoemaking business from 1825, employing one, two or three men up until 1871; two women worked as shoe binders in 1851. Thomas Billimore was still working aged 81, but the trade seems to have ceased after his death in 1876 and that of George Willis, who died in 1885 aged 84.[160] Modern crafts housed in the converted farm buildings of Dummer Down Farm included a cricket bat maker and cabinet maker.

Malting and Brewing

Malting and brewing were frequently undertaken in medieval households. Ale was an important part of a family's consumption. Evidence from 16th-century probate material indicates that a domestic-scale production existed in Dummer, with references to a malt house, malt mill and quantities of 9–12 bushels of malt.[161] This was mirrored in 1803 when sales particulars of Stephen Dicker's farm included a 30-gallon copper and brewing equipment – significant, but hardly commercial.[162] No other records refer to malting and brewing in the parish.

153 HRO, 65M72.
154 HRO, 65M72; 1827B/08; 1834AD/07.
155 *Census*, 1851, 1861, 1901.
156 HRO, 65M72; *Census*, 1851–1911.
157 *Census*, 1851, 1911.
158 HRO, AV769/128/S1.
159 *Census*, 1851, 1911.
160 https://www.freebmd.org.uk/cgi/search.pl (accessed 25 Jul. 2019).
161 Examples HRO, 1588B/51; 1599A/49; 1595A/32. A bushel is equivalent to 8 gallons or 36.4 litres.
162 *Hants. Chron.*, 21 Oct. 1793; 18 Apr. 1803.

Commerce and Services

From the mid 18th century to the early 21st century Dummer was served with basic essentials. It even had an estate laundry in the late 19th/early 20th century.[163] James Kinchin (d. 1748) was described as a grocer in his will,[164] and James Stevens was the earliest shopkeeper mentioned, in 1830.[165] John Budd may have taken over this business in 1837 and by 1841 was assisted by his son, a butcher.[166] The Englefield family ran a grocery shop alongside the beer off-licence at Tower Hill from at least 1867 to 1907.[167] A baker served the village from 1844 to 1907, when in the later years it was on the same premises as a grocer's shop and post office which opened in 1854 in Up Street.[168] James Allen (d. 1881) acted as postmaster as well as running his blacksmith, wheelwright and foundry business on the same site.[169] This cluster of services provided a small focal centre for the village. The grocery shop appears to have moved after Allen's death to Little Manor farmhouse in Down Street,[170] where farmer Rowland Davis Drinkwater took on the role of postmaster, grocer, baker and coal dealer.[171] At some time the shop and post office moved across the road to the corner of Post Office Lane and was run by Arthur Porter but eventually closed in 2006,[172] leaving the village with no local shops, Basingstoke being the nearest retail centre. In the 1950s Major Archie Coats supplied wild strawberries and employed local women to dress game birds from his shoots which were sold in London and France.[173]

The tithingmen's returns of the early 17th century stated that there were no persons selling beer in the parish,[174] but by 1839–41 James and John Stevens and John Barber were recorded as beer sellers.[175] William Tubb (d. 1858) owned and ran a beer house in a thatched cottage in Down Street where customers could drink on the premises.[176] Tubb's widow Mary (d. 1880) and daughter Charity continued the business and the cottage was altered and extended and bought by May & Co Ltd., brewers of Basingstoke, in 1893 and named the Queen Inn.[177]

George Page took over the licence in November 1899 but four months later he was fined £1 with £1 16s. 8d. costs for allowing drunkenness at the premises and his licence was revoked. Army pensioner Benjamin Bird Crofts took on the business in May of the

---

163 HRO, 10M57/SP375; 46M84/F69/2.
164 HRO, 1748B/063.
165 HRO, 65M72/PR5.
166 HRO, 65M72/PR5. *Census* 1841.
167 *P.O. Dir. Hants.* 1867, 515, and 1885–1907.
168 https://sites.google.com/site/ukpostofficesbycounty/home/england (accessed 25 Oct. 2018); above, Communications.
169 *Census*, 1851; *P.O. Dir. Hants.*, 1867, 515.
170 *Census*, 1881.
171 *P.O. Dir. Hants.* 1885, 651.
172 *Census* 1911; above, Landscape, Communications.
173 HRO, AV769/128/S1; Charles Palmer-Tomkinson, pers. comm., 2019.
174 HRO, 44M69/G3/145.
175 HRO, 1839AD/75; *Census*, 1841.
176 *Census*, 1841, 1851.
177 HRO, 97M83/XP140.

Figure 21 *The Queen Inn, Down Street.*

following year[178] and Frank Bone was registered as the landlord in 1939.[179] The Stonegate Pub Company owned the Queen Inn in 2020, which was run by tenants.[180] Also in 2020 a small outlet opened at the Dummer Down farm complex selling beer brewed at Breach farm in neighbouring Candover parish.

The Englefield family ran the Tower Hill off-licence and grocer's shop for over 40 years where customers could purchase a bottle or jug of beer to drink off the premises. On Henry Englefield's decease (1885) his son William took over the business which was purchased by May & Co. a year later, but the Englefield family retained the licence until at least 1907. They appear to have given it up when William retired.[181] The house was sold in 1950 but still retained the name of the Old Brewery in 2020.[182]

178 *Census*, 1841–91; HRO, 97M83/XP140.
179 *1939 Register*.
180 https://sotcd.co.uk/ownerList.php (accessed 25 Jul. 2019); below, Social History.
181 *P.O. Dirs. Hants., 1867–98*; *Census*, 1901.
182 HRO, 157M89W/2.

Commercial Developments

Redundant agricultural buildings were converted from agricultural use to office/commercial use on a number of farms. At Kennel and Clump farms they were converted to residential properties. Diversification at Dummer Down farm led to the redundant barn complex being occupied by a wide range of small businesses.[183] The fields around the farm were available to rent for camping, music festivals and as a wedding venue. This site was further developed in the 21st century, with new industrial units being built for small businesses.

The former stables at Manor Farm provided small office facilities but were empty in 2020. In 1978 the clock house and stable block in Kempshott Park were converted into offices[184] and a telecommunications provider employing 200 staff was based on the site of the former piggery at Glebe Farm which had been abandoned when the M3 motorway was constructed. Employees for these businesses came from outside the village.[185] The village also featured self-employed home-based businesses.

Figure 22 *Former coach house converted to offices, Kempshott Park.*

183 Below, Social History.
184 *Basingstoke Gaz.*, 1979.
185 Julian Jones, pers. comm., 2019.

When Basingstoke golf course opened in 1928 it offered new employment for some professionals and groundsmen from the village,[186] and a number of jobs arose when Dummer golf course opened in 1992 but few villagers were employed there in 2020. Since 2001, Tower Hill farmhouse has offered a bed and breakfast service. The former Methodist chapel in Down Street was an art gallery in the 1980s but was later converted to a home and office.[187] A specialist plant nursery operated at the former site of Oakdown Farm in Trenchards Lane opposite Ganderdown Cottages but closed *c*.2015.

In 1907 Charles Barnes described himself as a cycle agent but may have had his business outside the parish.[188] A map dated 1948 depicted a filling station adjacent to the general store and post office in Down Street,[189] run by Arthur Porter until the mid 1970s. Harold Hounsome purchased a property in 1926 at the top of Kempshott Hill in the north of the parish on the A30 which became a very successful petrol station and was bought in 1954 by Esso Petroleum. Adjacent to this was the Blue Hut roadside all-night café popular with bikers, run by Wilfred Appleton of Kennel Farm.[190] This started as a tarpaulin stretched between trees but upgraded to an ex-army hut, painted blue.[191] Both the Blue Hut and Kennel Farm were sold in 1964. The café was demolished in 1985 as part of the Beggarwood estate development where its memory is recorded in a road named *Blue Hut Way*. Close to this site a motorcycle clothing, sales and repair service was established in 1975 and still operated in 2020.[192] In 2018 a car repair garage opened at Oakdown Farm.[193] Highways England had a depot adjacent to the motorway junction housing offices, salt storage barns and equipment stores.

186 *1939 Register*.
187 *Conservation Area*; HRO, AV769/128/S1.
188 *P.O. Dir. Hants.*, 1907, 158.
189 HRO, H/SY/B1/A12/2.
190 Napier, *Kempshott Park*, 19.
191 http://www.trucknetuk.com/phpBB/viewtopic.php?f=35&t=12421&start=2250 (accessed 26 Sept. 2019); http://www.kempshotthistorygroup.org.uk/gallery/toll-roads-turnpikes-and-the-a30 (accessed 26 Sept. 2019).
192 http://www.mottmotorcycles.co.uk/about-us.aspx (accessed 26 Sept. 2019).
193 https://beta.companieshouse.gov.uk/company/08240982 (accessed 30 Nov. 2019).

Parish Studies of Agriculture after 1700

Local agricultural studies are a means of testing theories propounded by national historians for wider areas and land types. Mark Overton in *Agricultural Revolution in England. The transformation of the agrarian economy 1500-1850* (Cambridge, 1996) argued that from 1750 to 1850 decisive breakthroughs took place in output and productivity. Study of enclosure and new crops in Dummer can illustrate Overton's argument. The Enclosure of Dummer in 1743 redrew 80 per cent of the parish transforming it into its modern more productive form. Crop returns, available from 1801, revealed new crops. Other documents such as tithe maps and apportionments (1838), Ministry of Agriculture returns (1866-1931), and personal testimony show increased expansion of local agriculture.

In parishes where enclosure of the common fields and commons took place before 1700 it was often by an informal agreement and no record may exist. Some parishes may have been enclosed at a very early date and some may never have had open fields. The other records are common to virtually all parishes.

Parliamentary Enclosure

Landlords, the rector and substantial tenants often sought parliamentary enclosure to improve the efficiency of their farming by moving from scattered strips in the open fields to enclosed fields grouped into compact holdings. A bill for enclosure was drawn up and examined in a committee of the House of Commons. Permission was usually granted if the owners of four fifths of the land agreed. It was recorded by the committee that seven Dummer landowners refused to consent to the bill. Their reasons were not stated and they failed to attend the committee so the bill became law. If objectors did attend committees, very interesting discussions can be found in Parliamentary Papers.

Following the Act, an enclosure award and map were drawn up by surveyors appointed by Parliament. The surveyors tried to be fair. They viewed everyone's documents relating to land rights including copies of the manorial court rolls, and allocated fields accordingly. Any squatters without legal rights were not allocated land even if they had lived locally for a long time. In this award all roads, tracks, footpaths and new enclosures were listed with their extents. Provision was made for the planting or erecting of hedges and fences. This was all mapped (Map 7) giving a very clear description of the parish in 1743. Many enclosures led to the relocation of the farmhouses to the centre of the new compact farms and Dummer Down farm is probably one such example. In many parishes, some who were allotted small amounts of land found the whole process too expensive, especially as they lost common land rights, and sold up. Thus the social consequences of enclosure for the poor could be severe.

In some parishes, there was also a pre-enclosure map indicating the open fields and strips. This is not the case in Dummer but the shape and number of the open fields can be seen from the enclosure map of 1743.

Crop Returns

The earliest crop surveys were carried out in the mid 1790s by the government following several poor harvests and in wartime. The earliest for Dummer which has survived is the parish acreage return of 1801 where one of the crops mentioned is turnips. This was an important innovation in the 18th century popularised by Charles Townshend, nicknamed Turnip Townshend, who encouraged a four-field crop rotation of wheat, turnips, barley and clover. For the first time there was no need to slaughter animals before winter as turnips could be stored for fodder; fields no longer had to be left fallow and clover put nitrogen back into the soil, all resulting in increased harvests. Such innovations were much easier to achieve on enclosed fields.

Tithes

The clergy of the Church of England were maintained by compulsory tithes from the Middle Ages. Initially these were paid in kind in animals, poultry and their products, and crops. Over time some of these became money payments and in 1836 all tithes were commuted and tithe commissioners determined how much each occupier in each field of England had to pay. To make this assessment, each parish was visited by inspectors who reported on agriculture in the parish. These reports are retained in The National Archives. For each parish, the Title

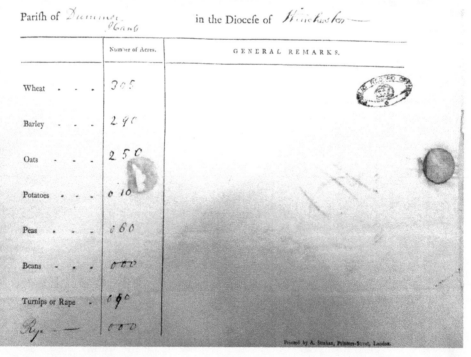

Figure 23 *1801 parish acreage return.*

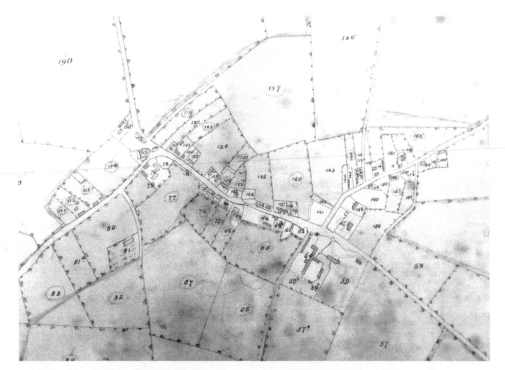

Map 7 *Dummer tithe map, 1838.*

Commutation Act of 1836 required a detailed map numbering every field and building plot accompanied by an apportionment listing size, tithe payment due, ownership, occupier and cultivation. These are the first nationwide indications of land use in each field in every parish but unfortunately the cultivation column in the assessment for Dummer, drawn up in 1840, has been left blank. This is very rare and unfortunate for the historian. Fortunately, when the Ordnance Survey mapped Britain by county and parish at a scale of 1:2,500 in the second half of the 19th century, the land use and area of every mapped parcel of land was recorded and published in the Parish Books of Reference or Area Books. These proved invaluable for Dummer as the 1838 tithe apportionment failed to record land use.

Ministry of Agriculture Returns

By far the most comprehensive continuous picture of parish productivity is from the parish reports to the Ministry of Agriculture from 1866 held in The National Archives which for Dummer are available from 1866 to 1981. The early returns record the numbers and ages of livestock relevant to their breeding capability. Surveys of 1875 and 1901 include the size of holdings and crop acreages.

When the Second World War began there was an urgent need to increase food production as imports of food and fertilisers were drastically cut. Between 1940 and 1943 a national survey covered every farm and holding over

5 a. These show the varieties of crops, animal stock, number of workers, condition of the farm, numbers of tractors and even pest infestations and were designed to bring uncultivated land into production. These are sometimes called the Second Domesday Book. Dummer is fortunate in having several correspondence files giving weekly accounts by the tenant of Village farm to his landowner describing the difficulty in running a poultry farm during the Second World War. These included land being requisitioned by the War Office. There were difficulties in buying birds, transporting them with lack of fuel, sourcing poor feed from army canteens and bakers' sweepings all with demands for payment in advance from hens going off lay and not generating an income. There was a shortage of employees, many of whom had enlisted or joined the manufacturing companies in Basingstoke.

Personal Testimony

Understanding farming in the 21st century requires talking to present-day landowners and farmers. The cultivation of Dummer's fields is a highly commercial business. The formation of a co-operative with neighbouring farms enabled the sale of out-of-date, duplicate machinery and investment in more efficient modern equipment. Although not farmed organically the reduced use of pesticides, national banning of neonicotinoids, set aside sowing for wildlife and a better understanding of biodiversity and carbon capture has moved ploughing through deep, minimum to zero tilling resulting in increased fertility, worm and insect populations. National awards for soil fertility were received in 2015 and 2022.

THE LIVES OF THE PEOPLE of Dummer and Kempshott were long characterised by agricultural labour. Lords of the manor(s) were usually resident and dominated parish society until the break-up of the estate in the 1920s. The parish's relationship with nearby Basingstoke has been influential, as have important transport routes traversing the parish. Major change occurred in the 20th century. What was a farming-centred society until the 1950s has become a prosperous commuter and retirement village. Dummer had a school from 1610 and a number of endowed charities. Social links with Kempshott were close long before it was added to the civil parish in 1879.

Social Structure and Character

The Middle Ages

By the beginning of the 14th century Dummer was in the middle rank of parishes in the Bermondspit hundred when compared for wealth, with tax assessed in 1327 at 41s. 11d.[1] Four men stand out as better-off residents among the 11 individuals assessed: Hugh le Franklin, whose name suggests that he was a free man holding his own land; the rector Nicholas de Middleton; Gilbert de Stainford;[2] and Thomas Preposito, presumably the reeve, overseer of the lord's estate. In Popham, a parish directly to the west, while 18 people were assessed for tax, the amount raised was only a modest 26s. 10d.[3] The effect of the Black Death on Dummer is unknown but was serious throughout the county. There appears to have been no devastating decline, as at neighbouring Kempshott, Farleigh Wallop and Hatch, and – like Cliddesden – the community's survival may have been at their expense, benefitting from rising prices, the greater availability of land and the growing cloth industry in the area.[4] The population of Kempshott was always small; the Black Death appears to have hastened its decline and by 1393 there were no residents in the parish.[5]

---

1   *Hants. Tax List 1327*, 41. South Warnborough was assessed at 79s. 10d. and Nutley at 14s. 1d.
2   Stainford translates as 'stoney ford' but no such place can be located in a parish without surface watercourses.
3   *Hants. Tax List 1327*, 39. Popham formed part of Micheldever hundred: *VCH Hants.* III, 397–9.
4   *Cliddesden, Hatch and Farleigh Wallop*, 45.
5   *Reg. Wykeham* II, 441–2.

16th–18th Centuries

In 1525 Dummer had 34 taxpayers.[6] Prominent residents included the Dummer family, lords of West Dummer. Henry Dummer (d. 1540) left three of his four children a tenement each and 140 sheep and six cows to be divided amongst them.[7] Probate material between 1519 and 1560 illustrates a wide range of wealth, sheep increasing the value of inventories and wills. John Grant (d. 1557) appears to have been the most prosperous parishioner during this period, whose inventory had a total value of £115 14s. 6d.[8] In the middle rank, Thomas Morrell's inventory (d. 1554) had a value of £43 10s. 10d.[9] The lowest value of an inventory was that of Christopher Bodicote (d. 1558) at £4 9s. 4d.[10] Wealthy parishioners at the end of the century included a widow, Alice Madgwick (d. 1591), who left bequests of £160, a gold ring, silver spoons and deeds to free land in Dummer[11] and Gilbert Wither (d. 1599), a yeoman and a member of the well-known Hampshire family of that name. Wither leased Dummer [Manor] farm and had an inventory valued at £956, of which £400 was the value of the 45-year lease.[12]

The rise in status of families such as Millingate and Soper is apparent from the later part of the 16th century onwards. John Soper (d. 1621) and John Millingate (d. 1626) were known as yeomen at the times of their deaths, while John Millingate the younger (d. 1655) and William Soper (d. 1688) grandson of John Soper were recorded as gentlemen.[13] William had bought land, farms and property in parishes in and around Dummer, as well as further afield in Hampshire and beyond. The value of his possessions must have been very considerable; the monetary bequests in his will amounted to over £1,200. The hearth-tax return of 1665 provides a picture of the social hierarchy of the parish.[14] There were 36 hearths of which prominent householders William Soper of the Grange had seven and Mistress Terry and George Ilsley, a prosperous farmer,[15] each had six. The schoolmaster, John Shipman, had three hearths and Ann Weston, a spinster, had one hearth. Dummer had the third highest number of hearths in Bermondspit hundred (total 158), figures ranging from two to 54. It also had fewer poor than most other parishes. Only five hearths were non-chargeable in Dummer as being below the rate on which assessments were made. This compared with 59 in Bermondspit as a whole.

Social relationships within the community occasionally broke down and villagers used the courts to settle disputes between themselves. In 1685 John Wake of North Waltham took a case in the consistory court against Dorothy Hall of Dummer in an attempt to defend his good name, Dorothy having claimed that Wake had raped her.[16] Mary Field of Dummer pursued Thomas Cooper, an innkeeper of Basingstoke, for defamation. She maintained that on numerous occasions in 1772 Cooper had said that she was a whore

---

6   TNA, E 179/173/183, rot. 13d.
7   HRO, 1540B/26.
8   HRO, 1557U/119.
9   HRO, 1554B/069.
10   HRO, 1558B/013.
11   TNA, PROB 11/79/174.
12   HRO, 1599B/50; R.F. Bigg-Wither, *Materials for a History of the Wither Family* (Winchester, 1907), 28, 69.
13   HRO, 1621B/50; 13M64/57; TNA, PROB 11/252/375; PROB 11/390/123.
14   *Hearth Tax 1665*, 218.
15   HRO, 1668A/046.
16   HRO, 202M85/5/7/4.

and a damned whore, that is that she had committed the sin of adultery or fornication.[17] The outcome of these cases is not known but they reflect society's outlook at the time that reputation was of great importance, economically as well as socially.

The consistory court was also used by the church authorities to correct parishioners' behaviour. Jane Hall had to perform penance for fornication in 1705, appearing in morning service in a white sheet and publicly repenting.[18] One wonders why Richard Soper of the Grange was charged to appear before the court in 1712 in a disciplinary matter; no information about the content or outcome of the case exists.[19] This court case follows earlier examples of conflict between the church and members of the Soper family and adds background to the unexplained high number of Protestant Nonconformists in Dummer recorded in 1676.[20] This level of dissent in a parish with a resident landlord, cultivated land as opposed to forest or moors and a nucleated settlement, factors that normally suggested religious conformity, is most unusual, the social structure offering no reasons for the religious differences in the community.[21] Indeed, dissatisfaction with the church may have been led by the landowners and leaders of village society, who held puritanical, Presbyterian views.[22]

Social as well as economic upheaval was caused by the enclosure of land previously held in common. The 1743 Enclosure Act allotted land to 17 people of whom Michael Terry, lord of the manor, was the greatest beneficiary, receiving 1,002 a.[23] This allocation amounted to well over three quarters of the parish – the whole parish excluding the Grange – and its enclosure transformed not only agricultural practices but working and social relationships.

1800–1939

At the beginning of the 19th century Dummer had a population of 286 and the lord of the manor exercised tight control over the activities of the parishioners and parish affairs.[24] By 1851 there were 402 residents living in 84 households, of whom 217 were male and 185 female. A high number of residents, 63 per cent, had been born in the parish. Others had come from the surrounding area with just 9 per cent born outside Hampshire.[25] Stephen Terry, lord of the manor, lived at Dummer House with his son Stephen, curate of Swarraton, Stephen's family and three resident servants. Terry's other son, (George) Seymer, farmed at Dummer Down where there were also three live-in servants. The Grange was occupied by a widow, Lucy Ewins, her daughter and one house servant, while the rector, William Adams, a single man, employed a resident housekeeper and servant.[26] Farmers occupied an important rank within village society, between the

---

17 HRO, 21M65/C9/288.
18 HRO, 21M65/C12/2/2.
19 HRO, 21M65/C10/3/51.
20 Below, Religious History; *Compton Census*, 83.
21 J. Broad, 'Parish Economies of Welfare, 1650–1834', *Historical Jnl*, 42 (1999), 985–1006.
22 Below, Religious History.
23 16 George II cap. 16, 1743; above, Economic History.
24 *Population Returns, 1801*; Byung Khun Song, 'Parish typology in early nineteenth-century Oxfordshire', *Agric. Hist. Rev.* 50.2 (2002), 203.
25 *Census*, 1851.
26 Ibid.

gentry and the general workforce, frequently undertaking roles such as overseers of the poor.[27] The majority of residents – farm workers or tradesmen – lived in estate cottages in the village or in tied housing on the outlying farms.

In 1911 the number of residents in the now combined parish of Dummer with Kempshott was 373, but the social structure of the community remained as stratified as it had during the previous century. Mobility, however, had increased noticeably, with only 37 per cent of residents born in Dummer. Of the 28 per cent born outside Hampshire, the highest number (8.5 per cent) came from neighbouring Surrey, Berkshire and Wiltshire, with the remainder having moved from a wide range of places within Britain and one from Germany. Sir Richard Nelson Rycroft lived in grand style at Dummer House with six resident domestic servants as well as daily and outside staff.[28] The 1926 sale of the Kempshott and Dummer estate saw the break-up of the old order, opening the parish to new and more varied ownership and interests. The Ferguson family purchased Dummer House and later Manor farm. They contributed much to the life of the village, which became the childhood home of Sarah duchess of York[29]

Rural Unrest

The riots and machine breaking that took place in the winter of 1830 across much of southern England – known as the Swing Riots – arose at a time of considerable economic hardship for agricultural workers. Discontent with wage levels, rent and tithe payments and inadequate Poor Law allowances was further inflamed by the introduction of what were seen as labour-displacing threshing machines. Richard Benham and John Paice from Dummer were apprehended for taking part in events at Wootton St Lawrence, Worting and other parishes around Basingstoke on 23 November in which money had been demanded from landlords and a threshing machine broken. They appeared before the Special Commission in Winchester and were admonished and discharged; many of their fellow rioters were committed to Winchester gaol. Farms in the parish escaped the mob's attention; however, the effects of the uprising lingered on, as depicted in a letter of 1832 from Stephen Terry writing from Dummer House on behalf of a family who originated in Cliddesden. He wrote to the Privy Council thus:

> Elizabeth Cook of this Parish with three children is invited by her husband James Cook under sentence of transportation for 14 years for rioting in December 1830 to embark to join him in Parramatta in New South Wales. The man is working for Mr Marsden the chaplain at that place and he has written and sanctioned the woman going out. I have prevailed upon the parish to advance her the money that is absolutely necessary I therefore beg the favour of you to advise me what ship she can go out in and at what precise time and from whence she must embark & what payments will be necessary and to whom paid. I should prefer her embarking at the Tower or River.[30]

---

27   Examples include Anthony Budd and Edward Cobden, overseers in 1861, HRO, 65M72/PV1; Tom
      Cooper, Grange farm, asst. overseer, *Kelly's Dir. Hants.*, 158.
28   *Census*, 1911.
29   S. Napier (ed.), *The Restoration of Dummer Bells 2011*, 48.
30   Chambers, *Machine Breakers*, 191.

Such petitions showed both a charitable wish to re-unite families and a desire to protect the parish against a long-term drain upon their resources in supporting the poor; a one-off payment for travel appeared a good investment.

Unrest continued throughout the decade and three cases of suspected arson took place in Dummer in 1833 and 1837. The first was at Henry Kersley's farm involving the loss of two barns, a cart house, rick house, granary, most of the corn and farm implements.[31] A few weeks later his windmill was burnt to the ground.[32] The third fire occurred in 1837, starting in the rectory barns that were full of unthreshed corn, and involved the loss of a stable, granary, hayrick, outbuildings and two valuable heifers.[33] Dummer was part of a national pattern of rural incendiarism in these years.[34]

1939–2020

At the outbreak of the Second World War most of Dummer's residents were employed in trades related to agriculture. Professional and government officers included the rector, an under-secretary of state for agriculture, an elementary school teacher, the sub-postmistress, a government officer (health) and a police constable. The first signs of factory work outside the village were evident with four men employed by an aeronautical instrument maker. Women were largely unpaid domestic workers in their own homes. Domestic service was limited to Dummer Grange, Dummer House, Clump House, the Rectory, Dummer Down Farm and Dummer Grange Farm. The national register compiled at this time identified 15 air raid patrol wardens, four Red Cross members, three special constables, a billeting officer and a Women's Land Army organiser, as well as the first evacuee.[35]

In 2011, the occupations and characteristics of people in the parish had changed dramatically. Of the 466 residents, 32 worked in manufacturing and the construction industries and the highest proportion, 57 people, were concerned with information, communication, financial and insurance services. Other large groups included 38 involved in the wholesale and retail trade and 51 people employed in education, health and social work activities. Not only had the move from an agricultural economy taken place but the status of residents had been transformed, with 69 people in higher managerial and professional occupations and only eight undertaking routine occupations. A majority of residents had been born in the United Kingdom (92.3 per cent).[36]

Gypsies and travellers were a group not always easily integrated into the community. In 1992 a gypsy and traveller site was established by the county council at Peak Copse, land between the M3 and A33, with pitches for 20 caravans and a warden's bungalow. It was temporarily closed in 1996 following some incidents involving violence, a decision upheld in 2002.[37] No authorised site for gypsies and travellers existed in Basingstoke and Deane district in 2020.

---

31 *Jackson's Oxford Jnl*, 4 May 1833, Issue 4175.
32 *Bell's Life in London and Sporting Chron.*, 9 June 1833.
33 *Hants. Chron.*, 20 Nov. 1837.
34 E.J. Hobsbawm and G. Rudé, *Captain Swing* (Harmondsworth, 1973), 324–7.
35 *1939 Register*.
36 *Census*, 2011; www.nomisweb.co.uk/reports/local area?compare=1170214313 (accessed 7 Sept. 2018).
37 HCC, Policy and Resources Policy Review Committee, 7 Nov. 2002.

Elite Social Life

Hunting was the sport of the gentry, described in the late 18th century 'as the pivot on which turned the whole social life of the neighbourhood'.[38] Meets of the hounds – there were five packs within easy reach of Dummer – followed by balls given in connection with the Hampshire Hunt (HH) were where the families of the neighbourhood met. The Terry family were amongst the Portals, Wallops, Knights of Chawton, Austens of Steventon, Digweeds, Chutes and others who were at every hunt and entertainment. In 1793 the Prince of Wales's hunting establishment at Kempshott changed from hunting stags to fox hunting, and it is fox hunting that occupies so much of Stephen Terry's diaries from 1841 onwards.[39] Sir Nelson Rycroft was master of the Vine Hunt from 1932 to 1938, following in the steps of his father Sir Richard Rycroft who was master from 1903 to 1913. Sir Nelson established the Dummer Beagle breed that hunted in the Vine, Craven and HH country until 1949 when he moved to Gloucestershire.[40] Shooting was another sporting activity; over 500 a. were advertised for shooting when Dummer House was let in 1881.[41]

Figure 24 *Hunting scene, watercolour by Stephen Terry, 1852.*

38   Stirling (ed.), *Diaries of Dummer*, 119.
39   Ibid.
40   J.F.R. Hope, *A History of Hunting in Hampshire* (Winchester, 1950), 137,168, 302.
41   *The Times*, 8 Nov. 1881, 14.

Stephen Terry (1774–1867), Diarist

The diaries of Stephen Terry give a perhaps unparalleled picture of Dummer life in the 19th century. Between 1841 and 1862, in a series of small exercise books, Terry recorded his everyday activities, hunting, agriculture, church life, village events, social life and visitors to the parish.[42] The editor of his diaries describes him as 'a typical English gentleman of his day … a remarkable specimen of the type and class for which he stands, Stephen Terry, squire of Dummer'.[43] Terry's studies at Eton and Cambridge were followed by an army commission. In Hampshire he served as a magistrate, managed his estate, brought up a family and indulged in his favourite pastime, hunting. The diaries portray a paternalistic society, with the squire and rector representing and upholding state and church.

Extracts from the diaries provide a flavour of Terry's social life, such as the entry for 12 May 1843: 'Picnic to meet the Smiths at Grange. After tea went on to a ball at Farleigh – got home by daylight.' Terry became related to the Austen family by the marriage of his son Seymer with Jane Austen's great-niece Georgiana Lefroy.[44] The Terry and Austen families met at assembly balls in Basingstoke and at balls in country houses in the neighbourhood. In January 1799 Jane wrote in a letter of a poorly attended ball with only eight couples and just 23 people in the room, of whom most were Jervoises from Herriard and Terrys from Dummer. She added the comment that the Jervoises were 'apt to be vulgar' and the Terrys were 'noisy'.[45] Terry lived at Dummer House, then at Manor Farm House and finally with his son Stephen, rector of Weston Patrick. He died the day before his 94th birthday in 1867.

Kempshott

Social life in Kempshott was transformed when in 1788 the Prince of Wales, the future King George IV, leased Kempshott House as a hunting lodge and established a royal residence outside London. He established his own hunt as well as becoming a member of the Hampshire Hunt. He built stables and kennels, which in 1791 housed 37 hunters and 80 hounds. The prince spent large sums on improving the house – built only 15 years earlier by Dehany[46] – furnishing it in a grand style and entertaining lavishly. Balls for over 100 people included members of the London court as well as the Hampshire aristocracy and gentry. Reciprocal entertaining placed a heavy financial burden on the neighbourhood, some of whom also became entangled in the prince's gambling parties in which £30,000 could be lost in a night. In 1792 his debts amounted to £370,000 and by the end of that year Kempshott had temporarily replaced Carlton House as his principal residence. The prince, whose marriage to Maria Fitzherbert in 1785 had not been validated, on the grounds that she was a subject and a Catholic, nevertheless brought her to Dummer, leasing nearby Southwood farmhouse as her 'official' home. In fact, the couple lived openly as man and wife, Maria describing these years as 'amongst her happiest'. Their relationship did not survive, however, and after his marriage to Princess

---

42   HRO, 21M49/1–22.
43   Stirling (ed.), *Diaries of Dummer*, 1.
44   HRO, 24M49/6: Austen, *Letters*, 490, 547.
45   Austen, *Letters*, 38.
46   Above, Landownership.

Caroline of Brunswick-Wolfenbüttel in 1795, the prince spent part of his honeymoon at the property, the end of his time in Kempshott.[47]

Edward Blunt and his family who lived at Kempshott (1832–76) exemplified the Victorian attitudes of benevolence to the poor while maintaining a rigid separation between the classes. A 'jubilee' event held in August 1854 for the club formed by the parishioners and friends of Dummer, Farleigh, Cliddesden, North Waltham and Popham and the hamlet of Kempshott to encourage the industry of the poor inhabitants, the production of the best vegetables, cleanliness of houses and general sobriety and deportment consisted of vegetable judging, games and races in the garden for the villagers, while the neighbourhood gentry were entertained to a 'most excellent cold collation in the house'. Miss Blunt returned from a continental tour 'to give her usual assistance in all matters of charity and amusement for the poor'. Stephen Terry lamented that 'the presence of the police on these occasions is always indispensable'.[48]

In 1866 Sir Nelson Rycroft came to live at Kempshott House, having purchased both the Dummer and Kempshott estates. At Kempshott in 1881 he employed a governess, butler, footman, groom, cook and housekeeper, nurse, two housemaids, kitchen maid, house under-maid, kitchen under-maid, nursery under-maid and a coachman. Outside staff included two gardeners and a gamekeeper. Sir Nelson lived at Kempshott House until his death in 1894, when the family then moved to Dummer House. Other residents of Kempshott in 1881 were a farmer, farm bailiff, agricultural labourers and their families and a coach builder. Sir Nelson Rycroft and his son Sir Richard Rycroft (d. 1925) fulfilled their roles in the parish not only as landlords but as churchwardens of All Saints' church and leaders of the local community.[49] Henry Gourlay, his wife and daughter Molly, who became a famous golfer, lived at Kempshott House before the First World War.[50]

Communal Life

Friendly Societies

Branches of two societies existed in Dummer designed to assist the welfare of the labouring classes: the Dummer district Labourers' Friend Society (LFS) and the Dummer branch of the Hampshire Friendly Society (HFS). The first organisation included in its aims the allocation of land for allotments to encourage 'cottage husbandry', established in response to the Swing Riots of 1830 and the severe economic conditions of the time, and the latter provided insurance in the event of sickness and an inability to work. A report of the annual meeting of both societies which took place on the same day in July 1861 describes a church service followed by a dinner at Kempshott House for 60 benefit and honorary members of the HFS who then met the LFS on the cricket ground where its members had organised a fruit and vegetable competition with 200 entries from 60 exhibitors, and both groups enjoyed the prize-giving and other amusements.[51]

47   Information in this paragraph relies on Golding, *Kempshot Manor*.
48   HRO, 24M49/11.
49   Below, Local Government.
50   *Hants. Chron.*, 15 Aug. 1908; *Census* 1911; below, Sport.
51   *Hants. Chron.*, 3 Aug. 1861.

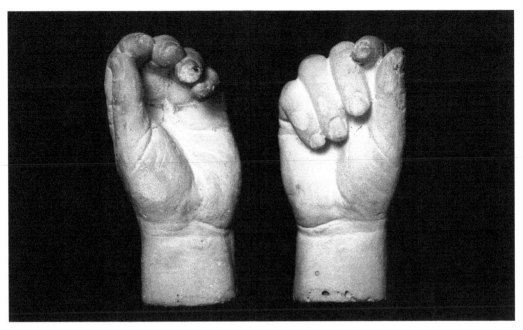

Figure 25 *Plaster cast of the hands of Joseph Arch (1826–1919), the first agricultural labourer to found a trade union and became a Member of Parliament. The hands may signify his background: 'To a labourer, life is lived through their hands.'*

The LFS was still active in 1882, when Joseph Arch, the president of the National Agricultural Labourers' Union, visited Dummer and addressed a meeting held in the Primitive Methodist chapel.[52] In the year ending 31 December 1902 the HFS had 55 assurance members and paid out £41 17s. 8d. in sick pay, leaving a balance of £52 10s. 4d. Sir Richard Rycroft was re-elected as chairman and Doctors Miller and Andrews were also re-elected at the Annual General Meeting.[53]

Social Activities of Church and Chapel

Church and chapel were the focus of many social activities in the parish. In the early 20th century the church choir enjoyed annual outings, travelling by train from Basingstoke to Bournemouth in 1903 and to London for a service in St Paul's cathedral and a visit to the Ideal Home Exhibition in 1908.[54] Church groups such as the Mothers' Union (MU) and Girls Friendly Society (GFS) provided regular social gatherings for their members and these also included outings. The MU were invited to tea at Kempshott Park by Mrs Gourlay in 1908, followed by a ramble through the grounds, and in 1909 they and the GFS were entertained to tea by Miss Rycroft at Downland House, Basingstoke.[55]

52   Ibid., 7 Oct. 1882; *ODNB*, s.v. Arch, Joseph (1826–1919), trade unionist and politician (accessed 9 Jul. 2018); above, Economic History.
53   *Hants. and Berks. Gaz.*, 21 Feb. 1903.
54   *Hants. Chron.*, 3 Oct. 1903; 15 Aug. 1908.
55   Ibid., 15 Aug. 1908.

The Belfry Club was active in 1970, meeting to ring handbells among other activities. Summer fêtes held at Dummer House or Dummer Down farm were part of the yearly calendar during the 20th century, a tradition continued in 2018 with proceeds usually shared between the church and the village hall.[56] Social events were very much part of Methodist chapel life, and from 1862 tea meetings and concerts were regular happenings. The circuit brass band performed in the village hall and out of doors.[57]

Reading Room, Village Hall and Women's Institute

An ex-army wooden hut purchased in 1914 and erected in Up Street as a village hall was renamed the Dummer Reading Room in a trust deed of 1927. It was a place of recreation for the residents of Dummer and Kempshott and provided books, newspapers and a variety of games, primarily designed for young working men. The wooden hut served as a village hall for many years but became increasingly dilapidated. When the school was closed in 1971 Sir Richard Rycroft secured £11,000 of the sale proceeds for the village hall. The Hall committee, chaired by Mrs Mitchell Innes, planned a new hall, incorporating a kitchen and stage, work starting in September 1973.[58] Improvements and alterations to the building took place over time and included full disability facilities in 2004[59] and new heating and the removal of asbestos in 2017.[60]

Figure 26 *Dummer village hall, built in 1973.*

56   As an example, *The Annual Dummer Fête and Dog Show 2015, Hill and Dale*, Aug./Sept. 2015.
57   Below, Religious History.
58   Ibid.; *Hill and Dale*, Sept. 1973.
59   *Basingstoke Gaz.*, 24 Dec. 2004.
60   Ibid., 18 Oct. 2017.

Following the closure of the post office and shop in 2006, a mobile post office was set up one day a week in the hall in June of the following year.[61] In 2019 regular groups meeting in the hall included the parish council, yoga, other exercise and dance classes and community coffee mornings; it was also well used for social and family events, with occasional plays and pantomimes.[62] These activities were disrupted in 2020 by the coronavirus pandemic, leading to temporary closure. The Clifton room built in the churchyard provided a venue for church-based activities.[63]

A branch of the Women's Institute (WI) was formed by Mrs Carlos Carey in 1942 with Mrs Hopkins of Village Farm as secretary and Lady Ferguson of Dummer House as president.[64] Dummer WI was established later than many Institutes in Hampshire, its foundation possibly due to a desire for women of the village to band together to help the war effort and to provide mutual support. Meetings were held monthly, and by 1949 there were 43 members. The WI supported the Analgesia in Childbirth Bill in that year and also completed the national village questionnaire, raising their concerns about the lack of electricity, mains water and sewage, the unsatisfactory arrangement of a public telephone kiosk which only had an extension line from the post office, the 'disgraceful' state of the WCs in the village hall and school and the 'expensive and over-elaborate design' of the new council houses, eight of which had been built since 1945.[65] Despite well-attended meetings, at the end of 1968 failure to find someone to undertake the role of secretary led to closure.[66] In 2020 a number of Dummer residents were members of the neighbouring Cliddesden WI.

Inns and Public Houses

Hostelries on the A30, the Wheatsheaf Inn, the Flower Pot Inn (closed in the early 20th century) and the Sun Inn, traditionally served Dummer residents but were situated on the north side of the road and were technically outside the parish. They provided meeting places as well as drink and food. The Wheatsheaf, an 18th-century inn now situated beside the Popham interchange of the M3, was a stop for stage and mail coaches on the London to Exeter or Southampton routes and acted as a meet for hounds in the 19th century.[67] In 1931 the Sun Inn, also a former coaching inn, added a tea room to attract charabancs and the growing number of motorists.[68]

Within the village the Queen Inn provided a social centre for the community. It started life as a thatched cottage in Down Street where, in 1851, William and Mary Tubb ran a beer house. By 1893 the cottage had been bought by brewers in Basingstoke, extended and named the Queen Inn.[69] In 2020 the Queen was a popular and well-supported village facility as well as attracting many visitors from Basingstoke and those walking the long-distance footpath, the Wayfarer's Walk, which passed its door.

61   Ibid., 13 Nov. 2006; 5 June 2007.
62   Lyn Hardy, pers. comm.
63   Named in memory of Colonel Peter Clifton of Dummer House (d. 1996).
64   HRO, 96M96/23/3.
65   Ibid.
66   Ibid.
67   HRO, 75A18/B22.
68   HRO, 10M57/SP377.
69   www.thequeeninndummer.com (accessed 27 Aug. 2018); above, Economic History.

Figure 27 *Molly Gourlay (d. 1989), golfing champion.*

Sport

Dummer had a cricket club from at least 1836, when a match was played between Dummer and Kempshott and a team from Basingstoke.[70] The team had a return match against Candover Cubs in August 1861 and was active in 1903, ending the season with a supper in the schoolroom.[71] Dummer Cricket Club had an extensive programme of matches in 2014 and continued in 2022.[72] A cricket centre was established at Dummer Down farm by Major Ronald Ferguson in 1995.[73] It was run by a sporting company, 'Serious Cricket', from 2009 and with three indoor net lanes, a playing arena and some of the best coaches in the county, it achieved a high reputation and recorded a 20,000 footfall in the year 2017.[74]

70   *Hants. Ad.,* 10 Sept. 1836.
71   *Hants. Chron.,* 10 Aug. 1861; 12 Dec. 1903.
72   *Hill and Dale,* May 2014.
73   Andrew Ferguson, pers. comm., Sept. 2018.
74   https://seriouscricket.co.uk/cricket-centre (accessed 27 Aug. 2018).

Two golf clubs existed in the parish in 2019. Basingstoke Golf Club had purchased Kempshott Park, excluding the house, from the Rycroft estate in 1927. A course was designed and built by James Braid in 1928 and Molly Gourlay, by then a famous golfer, having been a semi-finalist in the Women's Open in 1924, was amongst the official openers.[75]

Dummer Golf Course and Country Club opened in July 1992.[76] This was an 18-hole golf course on 165 a. near Kempshott Park and the Basingstoke golf course but separated from it by the M3.[77] In 2021 the Basingstoke club purchased the Dummer course and re-named it Basingstoke Golf Club.

Education

Pre-1870

In March 1610 John Millingate (d. 1626), lord of the manor, granted a house and garden for a school and master to instruct six boys from the poorest families born in the parish in 'learning and good life and also professing God's true and sincere Religion', as well as in writing, reading and grammar until the age of 14. After this they were to be apprenticed or employed in service as appointed by him and his heirs on the payment of 1*d.* yearly, if demanded. The messuage abutted Common Street (Up Street) on a site close to the existing pond.[78] The schoolmaster was to receive £4 yearly and the landowners were to nominate the children.[79] The first documented schoolmaster was John Shipman from at least 1655 and again in 1666.[80]

Other moneyed villagers in the 17th and 18th centuries made educational bequests. John Marriott (d. 1670) left £20 to be invested to raise an annuity of 20*s.* to buy bibles for three poor children of Dummer. The money was raised from selling the wheat grown in Bible Fields and any residue was for the remuneration of a schoolmaster. This bequest was still honoured in 1910 and possibly later.[81] Revd William Oades (d. 1731) bequeathed £2 10*s.* in perpetuity annually for the instruction of six poor children in nearby Preston Candover. However, if six months passed without master or dame, the money was to go to the rector and churchwardens of Dummer. It transpired that no money was paid to a master or mistress in either parish after 1746.[82] Peter Phillips was schoolmaster in 1714, followed by his nephew Benjamin Pointer in 1725.[83] In 1759 Thomas Henshaw of Bussock Court, Chieveley, Berkshire, inherited Fosbury farm (*alias* Bacon's farm) in Shalbourne, Wiltshire, passed down to him through the Weston family, of which one, Richard Weston

---

75 Molly Gourlay lived at Kempshott House from 1911 to 1915.
76 Plaque on club house entrance.
77 *Basingstoke Gaz.*, 15 Mar. 1991.
78 HRO, 10M57/K3. It was not until 1880 that children were obliged to stay at school until the age of 11, so Millingate's vision was ahead of its time.
79 Donation board in Dummer church.
80 HRO, 55M67/M29; HRO, 202M85/3/330.
81 HRO, 1670B/48; *Hants. and Berks. Gaz.*, 28 May 1910.
82 TNA, PROB 11/647/85; *Universities Com.*, 851–2.
83 HRO, 1714A/082; *Parson and Parish*, 45.

(d. 1600), has a memorial in Dummer church.[84] He bequeathed £10 for a schoolmaster in Dummer to teach ten poor boys and girls whose parents attended Church of England communion services. The master was to teach in 'some convenient place ... at his own charge and expense'. This clause was to cause a problem in later years.[85]

In 1807 there was an endowed free school with eight children plus six paying pupils.[86] Another endowment, Smith's gift (date unknown), left £25 in the hands of Revd Henry Worsley (rector from 1781) to generate an income to teach three poor children to read. This was passed to Revd Michael Terry (appointed in 1811), who added the interest that had accumulated and continued the investment.[87]

A new school building was constructed on the Up Street site by subscription in 1815.[88] By 1833 there was a National School with 40 children, 20 supported by endowments and a second school which opened that year with ten fee-paying children (details unknown), also a Sunday school attended by 36–40 children, free of cost.[89] In 1846 a house was built for the teacher through parish subscriptions and donations from the Education Department and the National Society.[90] The schoolroom was described as brick and flint measuring 28 ft. x 18 ft. (8.5 m. × 5.5 m.). The majority of the pupils lived within the parish but children from Kempshott, a mile away, were also admitted. There was only one schoolmaster and an unpaid assistant. The trustees were the landlord Stephen Terry; his son Stephen Terry, curate; Thomas Billimore, churchwarden; Revd Michael Terry; and Revd James Digweed.[91] Between 1852 and 1857 Mr Williams, tenant of Dummer House, ran a private school for 12 children,[92] and live-in governesses were employed at Dummer House and Kempshott House.[93]

1870–1901

An assessment following Forster's Education Act of 1870, which stated that elementary education should be provided for children aged 5–13, identified 50 children – including some from Nutley Wood and Kempshott who lived too far away from their designated schools at Preston Candover and Winslade.[94] The school building was enlarged and Frederic Sprigg appointed master, remaining in post until 1885.[95]

Sir Nelson Rycroft of Kempshott Park and the rector, Revd Sir William Dunbar, applied to the Charity Commission to take over Henshaw's Gift. This was granted on 20 February 1877 and gave control of staff appointments and religious instruction to the managers. The first two appointed managers were Sir Nelson and Richard Elwes of

84   TNA, PROB 11/690/248; http://www.asdguide.btck.co.uk/WindowsandMemorials (accessed 13 Apr. 2018); this bequest was synonymously called Weston's or Henshaw's gift.
85   HRO, 10M57/K3; H/ED1/2/32.
86   HRO, DC/M4/8/13.
87   HRO, 10M57/K3; *Charities Report*, 405.
88   *VCH Hants*. III, 360; *Charities Report*, 405; *Kelly's Dir., Hants.*, 1885, 650.
89   *Educ. Enquiry Abstract*, 842.
90   *Kelly's Dir., Hants.*, 1885, 650; HRO, 21M65/B5/2; TNA, ED 103/80, 47; *Hants. Ad.*, 12 June 1847.
91   Ibid.
92   HRO, 24M49/7.
93   *Census*, 1861, 1881, 1891.
94   *Rtn of Parishes*, 146.
95   *Kelly's Dir., Hants.*, 1885, 650; HRO, 65M72/PE1.

Dummer House.[96] In 1883 there were 107 children registered (average attendance 53).[97] The school received an annual government grant but by far the greatest financial support was from Sir Nelson Rycroft (d. 1894), with £90 in 1885 and amounts varying from £35 to £60 in subsequent years. He also covered the cost of repairs and coal for heating; his wife supplied needlework materials (at cost), as did Thomas Burberry the clothing manufacturer based in Basingstoke. Sir Nelson's generosity was continued by his son, Sir Richard Nelson Rycroft.[98]

The school was extended in 1893 and again by 1898, and in 1899 there were 77 children in attendance.[99] The schoolmistress, Ella Clarke, lived in the house attached to the school in 1891, but by 1901 the schoolmaster, Thomas Driver had moved out to Village Farm, probably because of the dilapidation of the house.[100] Revd Robert Everard of Dummer House gave private tuition to clerical students.[101]

1902–1973

In the early 1900s Hampshire County Council provided adult day and evening technical education classes in the parish reading room in such subjects as home nursing, cottage cookery and laundry. These proved very popular and had attendances of between 11 and 26.[102]

From 1903 to 1908 a dispute arose between Sir Richard Rycroft and the education department regarding Henshaw's Gift. A successor to the Fosbury estate, Alfred H. Huth, chose to withhold the £10 annuity, as he claimed that the charity had lapsed and considered that since the 1902 Education Act the county council had been responsible for the school. The solution was the creation of an education foundation scheme set up in April 1908 run by five trustees including the rector, the owner of the manor of Fosbury and a representative of the county council. The £10 annuity was awarded as an exhibition to Dummer children to continue to secondary schools or technical courses.[103]

In 1903 the school could accommodate 91 children (average attendance 71).[104] Pupil numbers were 111 in 1907 (average attendance 78)[105] but the First World War delayed any expenditure on the dilapidating fabric. An inspector observed that the attainments of the pupils were not high, with little differentiation between the work done by the middle and highest classes; infants suffered considerably from lack of freedom and were taught by imitation rather than natural conversation.[106] Subsequent inspection reports commended the high standards of discipline and attitude of the children[107] and creditable attainments in arithmetic, written English, reading, needlework and singing. In 1931 58 children were

---

96   HRO, 44M68/F2/154; TNA, ED 21/6354.
97   *Council on Educ.*, 661.
98   HRO, 65M72/PE1.
99   HRO, 21M65/B4/5; *Kelly's Dir., Hants.*, 1895, 131; *Parl. Grants*, 87.
100 *Census*, 1891, 1901.
101 *Hants. Chron.*, 12 Dec. 1885.
102 *Hants. and Berks. Gaz.*, 14 Apr. 1900; 21 Dec. 1901; 18 Jan. 1902.
103 TNA, ED 21/6354.
104 HRO, 48M71/16.
105 *Elementary Schools 1907*, 203.
106 TNA, ED 21/29331; ED 21/6354; HRO, 48M71/16.
107 TNA, ED 21/29331.

taught by two teachers in a single room suitable for just 49.[108] Three years later, standards were reported as poor, with teaching undertaken by a headmistress and an uncertified assistant.[109] There are no records in the Second World War that any evacuee children were registered at the school, which is unusual compared with neighbouring parishes.

Sir Nelson Rycroft (d. 1958) donated a field behind the school c.1949 for the benefit of the pupils and villagers. He charged a peppercorn rent of 1s. yearly but moved away in 1951 and after 1950 rent collection was forgotten.[110] The 1951 county development plan decided that expenditure on the poor structure of the building was not justified and that the school should close.[111] Three years later it was given voluntary aided status, leaving ownership of the buildings to the foundation managers. The parish council complained in 1959 that the managers, possibly anticipating closure of the school, were neglecting their duties. Electric lighting was installed in 1960 to replace oil lamps.

Closure of the school relied on available alternative accommodation, which took ten years to resolve, resulting in further decay to the fabric. The headmistress, Mrs Frankham, appointed in 1947, was praised for her dedication and for creating a friendly community. She retired in July 1971, which saw the closure of the school with just 48 children in attendance.[112] Pupils transferred to North Waltham school, as this shared the same rector as Dummer and Steventon.

Owing to a dispute over ownership of the field donated by Sir Nelson Rycroft, the school was not put up for sale until 1973. His son, Sir Richard, issued a deed of disclaimer transferring shared ownership to Hampshire County Council and the Winchester Diocesan Board. The site sold for £22,700.[113]

Social Welfare

Charity

A number of endowed charities were established to benefit the poor of the parish. In 1607 John Millingate, by deed, charged his close, called Leedgar's Close, and 9 a. of arable land lying in the open fields with 20s. annually for the poor, to be distributed at the south porch of the church yearly on 20 March. In 1905 half-crowns were given to eight recipients.[114] Michael Terry (d. 1710) devised his manor of Popham in Dummer and other lands in the open fields with 20s. to be distributed annually by the churchwardens at Michaelmas amongst the deserving poor of the parish.[115] This was said to be still happening in 1847, poor widows receiving sums varying between 1s. to 2s. each.[116] At an

108 Ibid.
109 TNA, ED 21/52202.
110 HRO, 128M96/C3/19; 44M68/F2/154.
111 HRO, 128M96/C3/19.
112 HRO, 65M72/PZ3; *Hill and Dale,* May 1972.
113 HRO, 128M96/C3/19; 44M68/F2/154; 77A03/7.
114 Charity reg. no. 237737–2 (removed Nov. 2004); *VCH Hants.* III, 360.
115 Charity reg. no. 237737–3 (removed Nov. 2004).
116 *Hants. Ad.,* 12 June 1847.

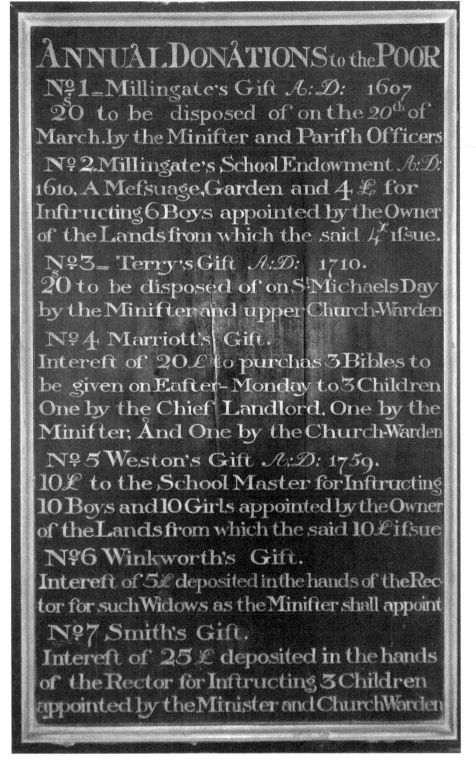

Figure 28 *Donation board in All Saints' church.*

unknown, but presumably later date, the Dummer estate still only paid £2 to a clothing club, the bequests of Millingate and Terry untouched by inflation.[117]

Adam's gift of £86 14s. 10d. consols, with the official trustees, provided that the dividends be applied in aid of 'funds of a provident club etc.' by a scheme of the Charity Commission, 31 July 1891.[118] The annual dividends of £2 3s. 4d. were distributed in coal. No copy of the scheme appears extant but the gift may have been made by the rector, Revd William Cockayne Adams (d. 1875). A 1929 statement of accounts of the three charities showed funds held of £22 6s. 8d. and that 2½ tons of coal had been purchased and distributed to inhabitants. The trustees of the combined charities were Revd A.J. Ireland, Sir Nelson Rycroft, Herbert Jones, solicitor, Montague Billimore, gentleman and clerk to the trust, and Kingsley Roberts, gardener. In a survey of small charities undertaken in 1967 by the Hampshire Council of Social Service, the purpose of Adam's charity was considered to be of a similar class to that of William Batchelor of North Waltham (provision of coal) and encouragement was given to broaden the terms and amalgamate the charities in order to be more effective.[119] The outcome of the review is not known but in 2004 the Charity Commission removed all these charities from their register. In 1847, a report of endowed charities in Dummer included Winkworth's Gift. This consisted of £5 given by a person of the name of Winkworth, the interest of which was distributed annually by the rector to five poor widows who received 5s. each.[120] Nothing is known of it after that date.[121]

In the 16th century charitable giving to the poor was perceived to offer benefits for the donors as well as the recipients. Roger Golde, rector (d. 1564), bequeathed 33s. 4d. to be given to the poor people of the parish at his burial, the gift to be repeated a month later and again at the next Easter after his death. On each occasion prayers would have been said for his soul. He also bequeathed a bushel of wheat and barley for every householder in the parish.[122] Nicholas Madgwick, clothier (d. 1566), made similar bequests of 40s., a quarter of wheat and a quarter of barley to be distributed at his burial, month's end and year's end and at other times as his executors thought best, for his soul's health and for his parents' souls and all Christian souls.[123] Alice Madgwick, widow (d. 1591), bequeathed £3 as well as 12 bushels of wheat and malt to be distributed at similar times and wanted 10s. to be raised annually by renting out 30 sheep; 6d. apiece to be paid to every household in the parish who could not afford to keep a plough – an interesting criterion for identifying poverty.[124] Other small bequests included two bushels of wheat and 20s. 'for the poor people.'[125]

The Madgwick family continued their support of the poor in the 17th century when in 1627 Walter Madgwick, yeoman, left 20s. for the poor of Dummer; Barbara Madgwick, widow, left 10s. in 1637 and Robert Madgwick, yeoman, left 10s. in 1651.[126]

117 HRO, 65M72/PW4.
118 Charity reg. no. 237737 (removed Nov. 2004); *Endowed Charities 1898*, 20.
119 HRO, 41M64/PK9.
120 *Hants. Ad.,* 15 Mar. 1845.
121 *Endowed Charities 1873*, 17; *1898*, 20.
122 HRO, 1564B/039.
123 TNA, PROB 11/48/417.
124 TNA, PROB 11/79/174.
125 HRO, 1578B/040; 1595A/32.
126 HRO, 1627A/31; 1637A/066; 1651A/34.

More substantial bequests were made by William Wither, former rector of Dummer, who left £3 in 1656; John Millingate, gentleman, who in the same year left £6 and his widow, Margaret, £2 in 1659; and William Soper, gentleman, who bequeathed 40s. in 1688. A few other gifts were made of sums varying from 2s. to 20s.[127]

Poor Relief

Statutory relief for the poor was provided out of the parish rate income which in 1776 amounted to £115 16s. 9d., of which £104 6s. 2d. was spent on the poor, including £9 5s. in payment of rent for housing.[128] Expenditure averaged £91 18s. 9d. in the three years 1783–5, rising to £325 18s. 4d. in 1803, an increase that was mirrored throughout the country largely due to price rises during the war with France. The cost of living and cuts in benefits were highlighted in 1795 by Anne Eggar, who with her two-year-old daughter received 1s. 6d. a week, whereas the payment had been 1s. 9d. a week. She claimed that 'the great advances in charges upon provisions and the necessities of life were insufficient for her future security'.[129]

In 1813, 26 persons were relieved permanently in their own homes, not in a workhouse, and 20 received occasional relief at a total cost of nearly £800.[130] This dramatically steep increase was followed by a drop to £342 in 1816 and then another peak, in 1819, of £614. The years 1818 and 1819, the period after the end of the French wars, saw high expenditure throughout the parishes in Bermondspit hundred, with Dummer amongst those spending the most. This reduced to £443 in 1822 and was then fairly static at about £500 a year until 1829.[131] In 1830, the year of the agricultural uprising when conditions were particularly severe, expenditure increased to £615 8s., figures such as this adding to the pressure for a reform of the system in an attempt to curb expenditure.[132]

From 1834 Dummer formed part of the Basingstoke Poor Law Union and paupers were sent to the union workhouse in Old Basing. The 1839 returns show the effect that the new Poor Law Amendment Act had in reducing the financial burden in the parish, with only £179 paid to the union.[133] In 1886 P. Budd and Edward Colden (Cobden), both farmers, were appointed overseers for the coming year at the Easter vestry meeting.[134] Overseers' accounts of 1927 show the poor rate collected to have been £851 9s. 6d., of which £542 was paid to the union and £240 to the rural district council.[135] Poor relief was renamed public assistance under the Local Government Act of 1929, which transferred responsibility for the service to county councils and county borough councils.

---

127 Examples include HRO, 1663A/114, 1679A/103.
128 *Poor Abstract*, 1777, 157.
129 HRO, 44M69/G3/790.
130 *Poor Abstract*, 1818, 402.
131 *Poor Rate Rtns*, 1825, 190; 1830–1, 179.
132 *Poor Rate Rtns*, 1835, 173.
133 *Poor Rate Rtns*, 1844, 153.
134 HRO, 65M72/PV1. Anthony Budd was at Manor farm and Edward Cobden at Village farm in the 1881 census.
135 HRO, 68M72/DU20.

Settlement and Bastardy

Evidence of settlement issues in Dummer are limited to the surviving records of settlement examinations, some with counsel's opinion. Four examinations took place in 1799, 1800, 1803 and 1810, with two removal orders into the parish, in 1761 and 1822, and one out of the parish in 1818.[136] This indicates relative stability of population. Three bastardy examinations were carried out in 1778, 1815 and 1831, the latter of a female child 'at the poor house', suggesting that the parish had allocated specific accommodation for poor people.[137]

Illness and Medical Help

Illness and accidents were never far from parishioners' lives. The death of Mary Holmes from what was presumably oedema reached the national press. It was reported that she had been 'tapped sixty times from July 1799 to January 1806, and had drawn off 4,153 pints of water'.[138] The rescue of a four-year-old boy, Alfred Bowman, from a village well in 1887 received wide coverage. The well was 258 ft. (78.6 m.) in depth containing 12 ft. (3.7 m.) of water. A 58-year-old labouring man, George Eales, took half an hour to climb down the rope and fix another rope around the child who was struggling in the water and for both to be drawn to safety. Eales was awarded the Royal Humane Society silver medal for his courage and coolness.[139] Sadly, wells provided opportunities for suicide; in 1761 Richard Geary, a blacksmith, lowered himself into a well with rope round his middle and neck.[140] The outcome of the inquest is not known but a verdict of lunacy was returned on Jacob White who was found hanging in a barn belonging to Thomas Terry in 1799.[141] The death of a Mrs Steptoe in 1855, described as 'a voluntary Pharmocognian and surgical attendant on the poor' and as 'a great loss to the parish', provides an indication both of unmet need and of the inadequacy of the informal help that attempted to fill the gap.[142]

Medical officers were employed by the poor law union and by the Hampshire Friendly Society.[143] Basingstoke Cottage Hospital opened in 1879, though its use required payment. The coming of the National Health Service in 1948 transformed medical help for many, although Dummer's rural location and facilities meant that access to services was difficult. In 1949 the nearest midwife who could administer analgesia was reported to live five miles away; informal help only was available for laying out the dead.[144] A welfare clinic was held in the village hall in the 1960s, closing in 1971 when the old hall was no longer available.[145] In 2020 Dummer fell within the area served by the NHS Oakley and Overton general practice.

---

136 HRO, 16M83/PO6/7; 16583/PO7/12; 19M76/PO5/147.
137 HRO, 44M69/G3/512; 3M70/60/17; 3M70/60/37.
138 *The Lancaster Gaz. and General Ad.*, 8 Feb. 1806, Issue 243.
139 Royal Humane Society, case no. 23,831, LMA/4517/B/01/01/015/23831.
140 *Public Ledger*, 31 Dec. 1761.
141 *Oracle and Daily Ad.* (London), 19 Jul. 1799.
142 HRO, 24M49/10.
143 B. Large, *Basingstoke Workhouse and Poor Law Union* (Stroud, 2016), 96; Drs Miller and Andrews, *Hampshire Friendly Society*, 1902.
144 HRO, 96M96/23/3.
145 *Hill and Dale*, Jan. 1968, Sept. 1973.

Diaries as Sources for Local Historians

Whether written for private or public consumption, a diary provides the historian with a direct voice from the past. It is a single voice, an individual view, a voice that is shaped by the society in which the author lived and by his or her position within that society. Attitudes and assumptions are revealed alongside records of events, great and small. Above all, diaries which record the life and activities of the writer's household and neighbourhood – whether kept as personal records or designed to convey opinions and influence readers – are primary sources of great interest when exploring the economic, social and religious history of a community.

The diaries of Stephen Terry (d. 1867) chief landowner in the parish of Dummer provide a panoramic view of mid 19th-century rural England. He paints on a broad canvas – from the minutiae of daily life in a small Hampshire village, to his passion with hunting and includes county affairs, excursions to London and news from abroad. Whether Terry expected or hoped that his diaries would be read by others or his daily detailed accounts were written for his own amusement is not clear. He showed seven volumes to Mr Harwood of Deane, a neighbouring clergyman, 'for inspection', but didn't say how they were received. The first volume was given to his daughter Eliza, and its whereabouts are not known.

Figure 29 *Twenty-two small notebooks containing Terry's diaries dating from October 1841 to March 1862.*

Victorian England was a time of enormous change, travel not least amongst the transformations that took place, with the introduction of steam power and the development of the train network in the 1840s. Terry's diaries reflect the time when in 1845 he rode on horseback to and from Devon, and the local means of travel for himself and his family included the prestigious Dummer carriage, a phaeton, which was an open, four-wheeled carriage drawn by a pair of horses, a two-wheeled, one horse gig, a pony chair – probably what he refers to as 'the basket' – and a donkey cart. In September 1855 he wrote of a new acquisition, 'I was allowed to name the little carriage Phenomenon (a wonderful work of nature) the little mare to be called Music, because her paces are like music. The carriage well suits two ladys and a child or two behind, does not suit bad roads.' The first mention of travel by train was in 1843 and outings to London and Southampton became not infrequent. In July 1845 Terry recorded a journey: 'by 9 o'clock train from Basingstoke to see the Queen on her yacht go out of Portsmouth Harbour at the head of the nine Men of War etc. A day ticket from Basingstoke–Gosport was charged only 13/6', and in April 1847 wrote of his son who farmed at Dummer Down, 'Seymer bought a black horse at Romsey Fair, the first time of traveling by train there.' Goods as well as passenger traffic proved beneficial, as in the very cold winter of 1855: 'February 8th, Three days snow again. The Teams will be in trouble to bring coals from the Andover [Road] Station, one load for the Penny Club.' Later that year Terry reflected, 'Steam may be used instead of cart horses … the principles of the endless railway will be so carried out as to effect large individual savings to the farmer and a great national importance to convert horse food to people'.

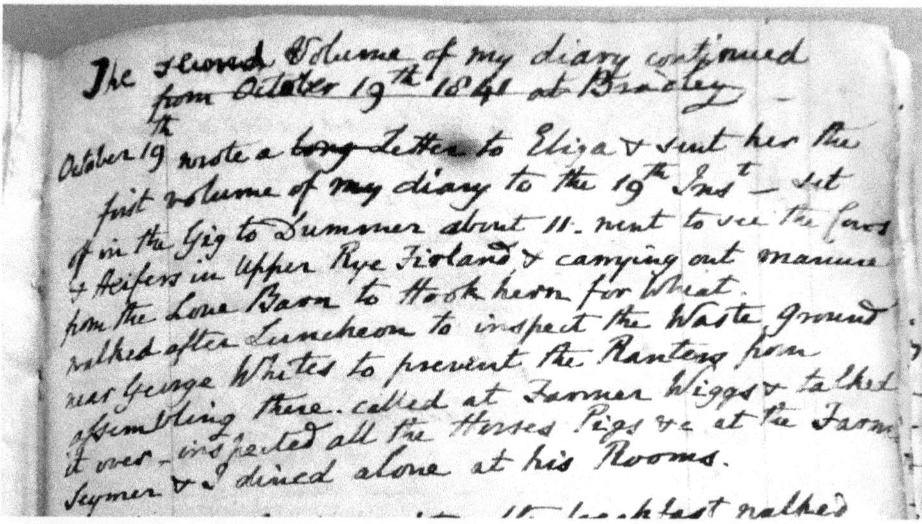
The second Volume of my diary continued
from October 19th 1841 at Bradley –
October 19th wrote a long Letter to Eliza & sent her the
first volume of my diary to the 19th Inst – set
off in the Gig to Dummer about 11 – went to see the Cows
& Heifers in Upper Rye Field & carrying out manure
from the Lone Barn to Hook heron for Wheat.
walked after Luncheon to inspect the Waste ground
near George Whites to prevent the Ranters from
assembling there. called at Farmer Wiggs & talked
it over – inspected all the Horses Pigs &c at the Farm –
Seymer & I dined alone at his Rooms.

Figure 30 *Diary entry for 19 October 1841. Includes reference to 'Ranters', a name given to Primitive Methodists.*

Continuity as well as change may be revealed in the pages of a diary; in the case of Terry his upholding of the social order and his admiration for royalty, the aristocracy and the gentry stands out. In June 1855 he wrote, 'Ascot without royalty either English or Foreign was a great drawback last week.' His description of each meeting of the hunt starts with a list of aristocrats and gentry, the Duke of Wellington often at its head. At one meet near Southampton, he was disappointed by the field, bemoaning: 'about 50 horsemen, not a very aristocratic meeting – but the exercise good'. In November 1854 Terry noted: 'A very aristocratic idea has been lately proposed to raise the society of this large County, particularly the northside, by the co-operation of the principal old County Gentry ....' He outlines the plan to form 'a Club meeting at Andover once a year in the hunting season with a dinner and a ball', the aim being to encourage the members 'to come forward on public occasions when the welfare of the County requires a large attendance'.

Diaries contain information unlikely to be found elsewhere. Who would have known of the move to rebuild Dummer's All Saints' church by the wealthy rector, William Adams? His offer of £500 towards the project in 1858 was not matched by others and the ancient church was 'saved' from Victorian good intentions. Diaries can intrigue, and shock, as when Terry's entry for 26 July 1855 recorded, '250 emancipated African negro slaves on their way to their purchaser in London were on the train yesterday'. Research shows that 48 freed slaves arrived at Southampton on the Royal Mail steam ship, *Tay*, from Havana on 22 July 1855 and were travelling back to West Africa. Diaries reveal the concerns of the day as well as the writer's own particular worries. Terry writes on hunting and whether the clergy should take part, and of the game laws in which over-zealous preservation of game appeared to outweigh the fate of offenders' children. His description of the burial of Sir Henry Tichborne (d. 1845) in the family vault of the parish church at Tichborne highlights the established church's attitude towards Catholicism, while the account of electioneering that took place among magistrates before the voting in of a new chief constable of Hampshire in 1856 reveals how appointments to public posts were carried out.

Terry's feelings for Dummer and for his family are apparent in his diary entries. He is pleased when visiting cottagers in 1847 'to see in every instance such neatness as well in the houses as in the gardens'. He is also pleased when 'the Dummer people' win prizes for fruit and vegetables at local events. On the debit side, instances of drunkenness, debauchery, wife beating and peculation led him to write in 1855 of the 'stigma' and that 'this parish is now notorious for instances of the kind'. His family, their health and activities fill many pages. The entry for 11 November 1852 shows Terry as a devoted grandfather: 'Rainy all day. I painted drawings for the children.'

RELIGIOUS HISTORY

THERE WAS A CHURCH IN Dummer in 1086, and documentary evidence from the late 12th century onwards reveals the long history of Christian worship in the parish. The church was independent from the Middle Ages and was served by a rector until the mid 20th century. In 2010, after a number of different groupings with surrounding parishes, Dummer became part of the United Benefice of Farleigh, Candover and Wield. The parish stands out from 1660 to the 19th century for its support of radical religion. A high level of Protestant nonconformity was evident in the second half of the 17th century, though in the context of the parish church. The parish had had links with John Wesley, co-founder of Methodism, and its incumbents were participants in the evangelical revival of the following century.

The small flint-walled church of All Saints has a 13th-century chancel and medieval timber-framing of the nave roof and belfry. A second church may have existed at Dummer – each manor claimed a church in 1086 – and that belonging to Kempshott was lost in the 14th century. A Primitive Methodist chapel existed in Dummer from 1862 until 1964.

Figure 31 *The church of All Saints showing porch, bell turret and south wall with Norman doorway, now a window, and added window in the gallery.*

Church Origins and Parochial Organisation

The Domesday survey records a church in entries for the manors of both East and West Dummer.[1] In 1275, it was agreed that the two manorial lords would henceforth take turns as patrons of a single church. There is no physical or archaeological evidence of a second church and it is possible that the claim made in 1086 was to the right of presentation rather than the existence of two church buildings.[2] The dedication to All Saints is first hinted at in the 16th century and may have been earlier. No alternative dedication is known. Occasional disputes over the advowson arose until the manors came into common ownership at the end of the 16th century.[3]

The earliest identifiable clergyman in Dummer was Geoffrey, son of Ralph Dummer, who was rector of the church in 1198.[4] Baptism, marriage and burial registers survive from 1541, an early date for such records. Changes to the boundaries of the ecclesiastical parish first occurred in 1931, when a portion of Winslade parish (Kempshott) was transferred to Dummer. In 1960 a small area of Wootton St Lawrence was added to the parish.[5] Until 1959 Dummer was served by a rector, at times assisted by a curate. In that year Dummer was united with Steventon and North Waltham – parishes lying west of the A30 – although it remained a distinct parish. This arrangement was dissolved in 1972 and Dummer was joined with Ellisfield and Farleigh Wallop, parishes to the east, to form a new benefice.[6] In 1983 a benefice was formed consisting of Cliddesden, Farleigh Wallop, Ellisfield and Dummer, sharing one priest and with a rectory house at Ellisfield.[7] This became a single parish in 2008, known as Farleigh,[8] and in 2010 formed part of a new united benefice of Farleigh, Candover and Wield with a rector and an associate rector, the latter holding primary pastoral responsibility for the northern parishes including Dummer.[9]

Advowson

It is likely that the advowson always formed part of the Dummer estate. In 1198 Geoffrey son of Ralph Dummer was parson of the church, and a half-hide of land in Dummer was given to him by his brother Robert, to be held in free alms by his successors.[10] Two generations later a dispute arose between Sir John Dummer and his cousin, John Dummer of Aston, joint holders of the manor, respecting the advowson of the church, and it was ultimately agreed in 1275 that the heirs of each should present alternately.[11]

---

1   *Domesday*, 108, 121.
2   TNA, CP 25/1/204/12, no. 19.
3   Above, Landownership.
4   *Feet of Fines 10 Ric. I* (PRS, 24), no. 144, 97.
5   HRO, 21M65/Orders in Council/Winslade, 1931; Church Oakley, 1960.
6   HRO, 45M84/4.
7   HRO, 21M65/Orders in Council/Cliddesden, 1983.
8   www.allsaintschurchdummer.hampshire.org.uk/parishoffarleigh (accessed 1 Oct. 2013).
9   Winchester Diocesan Office: pastoral scheme, July 2010.
10   *Feet of Fines 10 Ric. I* (PRS, 24), no. 144, 97.
11   TNA, C 25/1/204/12 no. 19.

A second dispute arose in 1509 following the death of the rector, Thomas Spycer. Henry Long and Henry Dummer both presented rectors, the matter settled in the latter's favour in 1510.[12] William Moore, *alias* Dummer (d. 1593), proclaimed patronage of the church in his epitaph.[13] John Millingate, who acquired the manor of East Dummer, presented in 1589 and following his acquisition of the manor of West Dummer the manors were united, and the advowson descended with them.[14]

A single turn was bought by Robert Worsley Esq., of Pidford, Isle of Wight, who presented his son Sir Henry Worsley Holmes LLD with the living in 1781. Apparently always an absentee, his place was served by a curate, James Digweed.[15] Following Holmes's death in 1811, the advowson returned to the Terry family, lords of the manor.[16] Subsequently the advowson was bought by William Adams of Thorpe (Surr.), later of Dummer Grange. He presented his son William Cockayne Adams in 1848 and was succeeded as patron by his second son, Borlase Hill Adams.[17] The advowson reverted to the owners of the Dummer estate with the coming of the Rycroft family in the 1870s. After at least two other patrons, the patronage was acquired by Sir Richard Rycroft by 1915.[18] In 1972 the advowson for the benefice of Ellisfield, Farleigh Wallop and Dummer was vested in the Winchester Diocesan Board of Patronage.[19] The advowson for the benefice created in 1983 was held jointly by the earl of Portsmouth and the Diocesan Board of Patronage.[20] Presentation arrangements established for the united benefice in 2010 gave alternate patronage of either the Lord Chancellor or the bishop of Winchester, the appropriate diocesan body, the earl of Portsmouth and Sir John Baring, acting together.[21]

Endowment

The earliest known endowment was a half-hide of land in Dummer granted in free alms to the incumbent, Geoffrey, in 1198.[22] The living was valued at £8 in 1291[23] but in 1342 the incumbent struggled to pay taxation of 50s. required by the church.[24] In that year, the endowment was listed as one messuage, a garden, arable pasture and meadow worth annually £3 3s. 8d. with the tithe of hay, other small tithes and dues worth £2 6s. 4d. a year.[25] In 1535 it was assessed at £13 12s. 3d.[26] A large and unexplained increase in value was recorded in 1696 when a terrier of glebe land belonging to the parsonage of

12   Reg. Fox II, 19v.; Fox II, 20.
13   Below, The Church of All Saints.
14   Reg. Cooper, 13; above, Landownership.
15   *Doing the Duty,* 37–8.
16   HRO, 21M65/E2/249, Thomas Terry presented Michael Terry in 1811.
17   HRO, 35M48/6/1467; 35M48/6/1785; 35M48/1903.
18   *Kelly's Dir. Hants.* 1915, 181.
19   HRO, 45M84/4.
20   HRO, 21M65/Orders in Council/Cliddesden.
21   Winchester Diocesan Office: pastoral scheme, July 2010.
22   *Feet of Fines 10 Ric. I* (PRS, 24), no. 144, 97.
23   *Tax Eccl.* 212. By contrast Steventon was assessed at £10 and Cliddesden at £5 6s. 8d.
24   *Nonarum Inquisitiones,* 121.
25   Ibid.
26   *Valor Eccl.* II, 14; *Reg Gardiner,* 3v., appx. 4, 159.

Dummer identified 58 a. of land scattered throughout the common fields of the parish, as well as 5 a. of enclosed land, the parsonage house, barns, stables, well house, a number of cottages and commons belonging to the glebe land that supported 60 sheep, six cows and a bull.[27] At enclosure in 1743 one allotment containing 78 a. 1 r. 11 p. was allocated to Revd Thomas Stockwell in lieu of his glebe lands, cow and sheep commons.[28] An exchange of a small area of land was agreed in 1878 by the Tithe Commissioners[29] and in 1911 glebe land of 79 a. was sold by the rector George Jones, then bankrupt, to trustees (H.C. Howard, Revd R.N. Rycroft and the Hon. R.G. Wallop) for £1,240.[30] The tithe award of 1838 commuted payment of tithes to £472 11s. 11d. a year (including the tithe of glebe of £28 17s.)[31] The income of rectors was £337 14s. 1d. in 1898, which included £45 rent of glebe land,[32] and £387 gross in 1914.[33]

Figure 32 *The former Rectory, built in 1850, during renovations in 1972.*

27   HRO, 21M65/E15/32.
28   HRO, 10M54/A7.
29   HRO, 34M95/3.
30   HRO, 26M75/14.
31   HRO, 10M57/SP367; 334M95/3.
32   HRO, 21M65/B4/5.
33   HRO, 21M65/B4/6/6.

A messuage belonging to the rector was recorded in 1342.[34] The rectory built in 1850 at a cost of £1,800 replaced a previous house on the site on the other side of the road from the church, quite possibly occupying the site of the messuage recorded in the 14th century.[35] This substantial stone and flint dwelling in the Tudor style was designed by architect W.J. Dunthorn.[36] Standing in its own grounds of nearly 3 a., the house was described in 1881 as having a large entrance hall, dining room, drawing room and study, a good kitchen, scullery and domestic offices. On the upper floor were four bedrooms, two dressing rooms and two servants' bedrooms. The stables accommodated four horses and there was a coach house and chaise house.[37] Ownership of the rectory house changed hands a number of times but it remained as the parsonage house until the death in 1959 of Arthur Ireland, the last rector of Dummer.[38] Its size and cost of maintenance had become an increasing burden so that the creation of the new benefice with the rectory house at North Waltham offered a fortuitous solution to this problem.[39]

Religious Life

The Middle Ages to the Reformation

Three members of the Dummer family were among the early known rectors of Dummer: Geoffrey in 1198, John in 1304 and another John in 1334.[40] Nicholas Gervays of Middleton, known as Nicholas Middleton, was presented to the church in November 1315 and instituted in the person of his proctor, Thomas of Meonstoke.[41] He was later ordained deacon in March 1316.[42] A clergyman of some note, in 1325 Middleton acted as a commissary of the bishop, carrying out various duties on his behalf.[43] In the same year he leased former lands of the alien priories of Freshwater and Arreton on the Isle of Wight, which had been confiscated during the War of St Sardos (1324–5).[44] In 1330 Middleton exchanged benefices with Edward de Marleburgh, rector of Tidworth.[45] Richard Smith was instituted in 1342 and Robert atte Moure was rector in 1349.[46] Then, following the disastrous years of the Black Death, nothing is known until 1392 when Thomas Knight became rector.[47] Knight was followed first by John Reneway, Nicholas Brygges and John Edmunde and then, in 1450, by Thomas Halle, bachelor of theology, the first known rector to hold a degree.[48] Halle's stay was brief and on

34   *Nonarum Inquisitiones*, 121.
35   HRO, 21M65/B5/2; 10M57/SP367.
36   Pevsner, *North Hampshire*, 240.
37   HRO, 21M65/A2/5, 62, 63; 10M57/SP374.
38   HRO, 10M57/SP374; 101M81/12.
39   HRO, 21M65/B4/8.
40   *Feet of Fines 10 Ric. I* (PRS, 24), no. 144, 97; Reg. Pontoise I, 177, f. 45v; *Reg. Stratford* I, 439; 139v.
41   *Reg. Woodlock* II, 744, f. 21.
42   *Regs Sandale and Asserio*, 424.
43   *Reg. Stratford* I, 301, 94v; 320, 1028.
44   *Reg. Stratford* II, 621, 1612; *VCH Hants.* II, 230–1.
45   *Reg. Stratford* I, 380, 1257.
46   HRO, 44M69/C118.
47   *Reg. Wykeham* I, 22A.
48   *Reg. Wykeham* I, 200; HRO, 44M69/C4; Reg. Waynflete I, 28v.

his resignation the following year he was succeeded by James Blakedon, bishop of Accaden (Achonry, Co. Sligo, Ireland), who served as suffragan to the bishops of Salisbury, Wells, Exeter and Worcester between 1442 and 1453.[49] James was presented by Sir John Chaleers.[50] This was an unsettled period, with William Balton, *alias* Calverhull(e), spending just two years at Dummer before exchanging benefices with Roger Grey of St Lawrence, Winchester, and succeeded by John Argentyne, who was deprived for non-residence.[51] Some stability returned with the appointment of Thomas Spycer in 1488, who remained rector until his death in 1509.[52] On Spycer's death the two manorial lords each made an appointment: Henry Long(e) presented Michael Huntbache and Henry Dummer presented Richard Lamball BA.[53] These claims were disputed and Lamball was eventually confirmed in 1510.[54]

Church life and the involvement of the laity before the Reformation may, perhaps, best be judged by the fabric of the church remaining from that period, mostly in the nave, by the devotion shown by parishioners in gifts made to the church and by statements of faith found in surviving wills. These show a traditional Catholic religious community. A request by Henry Dummer (d. 1540) for 'my body to be buried in the church of Dummer in front of the image of All Saints' suggests the importance attached to a painting or sculpture and is a strong indication that the dedication of the church to All Saints was the dedication in place at that time.[55] Henry left 12*d.* to the mother church, Winchester cathedral, and a cow to the church of Dummer.[56] Such gifts were replicated by others, with evidence from wills dating from 1517, and included a newly built house, sheep – some specifically for the high altar and the rood light – as well as money for repairs of the church. Agnes Carter (d. 1528) bequeathed her 'soul to Almighty God and to Our Lady Saint Mary and to all the holy company of Heaven' and asked that her executors should remember her with a mass at the church of Dummer once a year as long as they lived.[57]

Reformation Onwards

Roger Golde MA, Oxon,[58] was rector of Dummer from 1524 to 1564, a span of 40 years and a time of great religious change. Evidence from the wishes expressed by many testators for their souls accord with the changing beliefs or laws of the time, either Catholic or Protestant, suggesting at least outward conformity within the parish.[59] Golde's will, however, proved in 1564, shows something of both traditions. It harks back to pre-Reformation Catholic beliefs with a gift at his burial of 33*s.* 4*d.* to the poor of the parish, the gift to be repeated a month later and again at the next Easter after his death. The bequest of a carpet, a cloth covering that lay on his bed, on condition that the church might borrow it

---

49 *Handbook of British Chronology* (ed. E.B. Fryde, D.E. Greenway, S. Porter, I. Roy), 3rd edn, 329. We owe our thanks to Dr John Jenkins for this reference and identification.

50 Reg. Waynflete I, 39v.

51 Reg. Waynflete I, 59v., 75v., Reg. Courtney, 39.

52 Reg. Courtney, 39.

53 Reg. Fox II, 15, 20.

54 Reg. Fox II, 19v.

55 HRO, 1540B/26.

56 HRO, 1540B/26.

57 HRO, 1528B/11.

58 *Alumni Oxon.* II, 59. No college given. MA 1520–1; Reg. Fox V, 98.

59 Dummer probate material, 1500–1570.

to lay upon the communion table at high feasts also suggests earlier practices.[60] Yet Golde asked that his body be buried before the pulpit in Dummer church, indicating, it would seem, a Protestant belief in the pre-eminence of the ministry of the Word. Golde's wish for burial was granted: a tablet marks his tomb at a pew's end in the nave.

Another long-serving rector followed Golde, William White LLB, graduate of New College, Oxford (d. 1588). His views were clear; in his will he declared his faith in Jesus Christ, seeking to be part of the 'elect and chosen in his kingdom', indicative of Calvinistic theology, and asked to be buried 'on the south side of the chancel in my parish church of Dummer near to the wall above the graces where I do attend'.[61] Two rectors at the beginning of the 17th century took an active interest in education as well as in their parish duties. Richard Marriott MA, rector from 1600 to 1624, spent two years (1606–8) as master of the Holy Ghost school in Basingstoke for which he was paid £12 a year; among his inventory were books worth £20.[62] William Wither who succeeded Marriott was a fellow of St Mary's College, Winchester (Winchester College), where he died in 1656. Besides a gift to the poor of Dummer, he left £5 for books for the college library.[63] There was no recorded Roman Catholicism in the parish during the 17th century, such nonconformity as there was being of a Protestant nature.

Dissatisfaction began to be expressed by parishioners during the long tenure of Hugh Davis LLB (1656–94). Davis, the son of a cook at Winchester College, a fellow of New College, Oxford, and – after the Restoration – chaplain to George, duke of Buckingham, was described as being 'very conformable to the governance of the church' and was apparently not to the liking of those in Dummer who wished to maintain Presbyterian traditions.[64] Davis became rector in 1656, although whether he was resident or left the care of the parish to Henry Smith, curate since at least 1642, is not known.[65] The religious views of the Millingate family, lords of the manor, appeared to have accorded with those of the curate and would doubtless have influenced others in the parish. Margaret Millingate of Dummer Grange mentioned 'Henry Smith minister' in her will of 1659, as had Robert Madgwick (d. 1651), a yeoman, who wrote of him as 'my minister'.[66] Margaret's will and those of John Marriott (d. 1670), William Soper (d. 1688) and Margaret's daughter, Amy Soper (d. 1701), all contain strong expressions of personal faith and expectation of resurrection. Hugh Davis or Davys was formally instituted as rector in 1661 and William Wells had replaced Henry Smith (d. 1661) by 1663.[67] Why Davis was selected when his views did not accord with those of the patron and parishioners is not known.

No evidence exists of meeting houses in the parish at this time and in 1664 there was just one case, that of Ann Weston, a spinster, who was accused of not coming to church and was presented to the archdeacon as a sectary.[68] It is therefore surprising that when in 1676 a national survey was undertaken of religious adherence 38 parishioners were

---

60   HRO, 1564B/039.
61   HRO, 1588B/73.
62   Baigent and Millard, *Basingstoke,* 143; HRO, 1624AD/088.
63   HRO, 312M87/E10/4; 312M87/E10/6.
64   Wood (ed. Bliss), *Athenae Oxon.* IV, 545; HRO, 202M85/3/330. Bingley, *Hampshire.*
65   *Alumni Oxon.* I, 380.
66   HRO, 1651A/34.
67   HRO, 35M48/5/1; 21M65/B1/35; 65M72/PR1 (possibly 1660).
68   HRO, 202M85/3/329.

recorded as Protestant Nonconformists with only 49 conformists.[69] This figure of 41.66 per cent places Dummer in an extraordinary light when compared with other parishes in the Basingstoke deanery. Crondall, second to Dummer in number of Nonconformists, had 27 Presbyterians and 470 conformists, while Basingstoke itself had just ten Protestant Nonconformists and 1,580 conformists.[70] Numbers of Protestant Nonconformists presented in this period for non-attendance at church are relatively low. It is likely that Davis, a high-church Anglican, described his Presbyterian-inclined parishioners as Nonconformists in 1676 despite them attending church.

There seems to have been a long-standing conflict between the rector and some of his more prominent parishioners. It is known that discontent continued after 1676. In 1684 Thomas Wither and Philip Soper were accused of non-attendance at church over a three-week period.[71] In 1686 William Soper, his wife and son, James Wigg and his wife and Henry Tribe refused to take communion on Easter Sunday – the most important festival in the Christian year – a clear and public statement of their disapproval of the church's preaching and practices.[72] Three years later, in 1691, Philip Soper was one of three parishioners who took action in the Consistory court against the rector, Hugh Davis, for non-residence, and this was heard on appeal in the Court of Arches, Westminster.[73] Soper of Dummer Grange and the Wigg family, who occupied a large area of land, were important village figures. How long Hugh Davis was absent is not known, but there were a number of curates in the parish during his incumbency.[74] Not all the curates were considered satisfactory: in 1692 Thomas Pryor was presented for not being sufficient for the cure and for serving without licence.[75] The 20s. that Margaret Millingate left the church was the only gift made to the church which appears in wills that survive from 1650 to 1700.[76] In 1670 John Marriott left an endowment for the provision of bibles for poor children in Dummer, as well as in Upper Wallop and Wantage (Berks.), but no gift for the church.[77]

Thomas Terry BA, graduate of New College, Oxford, was the first member of the Terry family, lords of the manor and patrons of the church from the mid 17th century, to serve as rector, his incumbency lasting from 1694 to 1721.[78] Terry (d. 1723) asked to be buried in the churchyard at Dummer. He left his eldest son Thomas his lands and property, from which he was to pay £500 to each of his four younger children. John Dobson DD, also of New College, Oxford, who followed Terry, became warden of St Mary's College, Winchester, from 1724 to 1730; parish duty was undertaken by a succession of curates.[79] William Oades held brief office in 1730, dying in the same year. He left money for the education of six poor children in Preston Candover, where he had been rector for 40 years,

69 *Compton Census*, 83.
70 R. Johnson, *Protestant Dissenters in Hampshire* (unpubl. PhD thesis, Univ. of Winchester, 2013).
71 HRO, Q9/1/18.
72 HRO, 202M85/3/333.
73 LPL Arches/Bbb/749,757. The result is not known.
74 Above, William Wills or Wells, recorded 1663, 1668, 1670, 1672, 1677, 1680; John Tipping, recorded 1662; Richard Walton, 1692: https://theclergydatabase.org.uk/, location no. 14824 (accessed 26 Jan. 2022).
75 HRO, 202M85/3/334.
76 Dummer probate material 1500–1700.
77 HRO, 1670B/48.
78 HRO, 21M65/B1/61/1.
79 *Alumni Oxon*. I, 408; HRO, 21M65/B1/67; 21M65/B1/66.

and in default, for six poor children in Dummer.[80] The remainder of his estate he left to the master and fellows of Pembroke College, Oxford, his alma mater. In a codicil he left gifts to the poor in Dummer and for coal and wood for prisoners for debt in Winchester gaol.[81]

Evangelical Revival

The evangelical revival, an 18th-century movement that emphasised the 'experiential dimension' of the Christian faith and the need for personal conversion, breathed new life into both the established and Nonconformist churches of the country.[82] Charles Kinchin, a fellow of Corpus Christi College who became rector in 1736, was a member of the Wesley brothers' 'Holy Club' at Oxford and, as his diary records, John Wesley visited Dummer from 3 to 18 April 1738.[83] Wesley preached in Dummer church at a time when many churches would not admit him to their pulpits. In consequence, Wesley often held meetings in the open air in an effort to take religion to the people, particularly 'the neglected poor'. In February 1739 Kinchin annoyed the rector of Basingstoke, Revd Thomas Warton, by preaching to a large crowd at the Crown Inn in the town 'where he prayed much extempore and expounded after the manner of the Methodists, taking a whole chapter for his text'. Warton complained that 'Inns were licensed to sell ale and other liquors ... but for no other purpose whatsoever'.[84]

Figure 33 *George Whitefield (1714–70) by John Wollaston, c.1742.*

Figure 34 *James Hervey (1775–1858) after J.M. Williams.*

80   Above, Social History.
81   TNA, PROB 11/647/85.
82   D. Shorney, *Protestant Nonconformity and Roman Catholicism* (London, 1996), 23.
83   www.visionofbritain.org.uk/travellers/J_Wesley/28#pn_27 (accessed 5 Sept. 2017).
84   BTH, 546–7.

In 1736 Revd George Whitefield (1714–70), who became a noted preacher on both sides of the Atlantic, spent parts of November and December in Dummer.[85] His first biographer (1772) declared: 'This was a new sphere of action among the poor, illiterate people; but he was soon reconciled to it, and thought he reaped no small benefit by conversing with them.'[86] Wesley gave a more positive and less patronising account of the parishioners when he recorded a visit in March 1739 and preached on Sunday morning 'to a large and intelligent congregation.'[87] Another clergyman equally famous in his time, James Hervey, author of *Meditations and Contemplations* (1746–7) and said to be 'one of the most widely read writers of the evangelical revival', was curate in Dummer from 1739 to 1741.[88] His 'description and beautiful account of Dummer and the adjacent country' was printed as one of a series of letters.[89]

The everyday life of the church during the time of revival and beyond is portrayed by churchwardens' accounts, extant from 1731.[90] Among the many entries for repairs of the roof, the tower, floor tiling and the like are purchases of books – a *Common Prayer* book in 1733 costing 15*s*. 9*d*., a Register book in 1741 for £2 2*s*., a copy of the *Act against Swearing* in 1746 for 6*d*. and a book for the clerk in 1775 at 2*d*. Thomas Stockwell, rector from 1742, served for nearly 40 years. During his tenure the bells were mended in 1745, a repair undertaken in 1759, and bell ropes were replaced at frequent intervals; one of the most interesting entries refers to the insertion of a window in the gallery in 1769 at the cost of £1 1*s*. 0*d*.[91]

19th Century

Non-resident clergy and those holding more than one benefice in the 'long 19th century' have been subject to criticism and Dummer was among those parishes where this practice existed. Henry Worsley remained on the Isle of Wight throughout his time as rector, from 1784, during which time James Digweed, resident curate, inhabited Dummer rectory. Worsley became vicar of Arreton, Isle of Wight, in 1791 holding both livings in plurality until his death in 1811 and having succeeded to a baronetcy as Sir Henry Worsley Holmes in 1805.[92] Michael Terry followed as rector and he too was frequently non-resident, with Michael Terry junior, his curate, resident in the glebe house.[93] Terry was also minister of Wield, around three miles to the south.[94] William Cockayne Adams LLD, of Balliol College, Oxford, was rector from 1848 until his death, unmarried, in 1875. He was ill in 1856 and again in 1861; unable to carry out his duties, he moved to live in Wisbech (Cambs.).[95] Stephen Terry, son of Stephen Terry the diarist (1774–1867) was curate from 1856 and required to live in the parish.[96]

85 *ODNB*, s.v. Whitefield, George (d. 1770), Calvinistic Methodist leader (accessed 6 Aug. 2017).
86 J. Gillies, *Memoirs of the Life of the Rev. Mr George Whitefield* (London, 1722), 11.
87 E. Stokes (eds B. & B. Applin), *The Making of Basingstoke* (BHAS, 2008), 155.
88 *ODNB*, s.v. Hervey, James (d. 1758) Church of England clergyman and writer (accessed 6 Aug. 2017).
89 Bingley, *Hampshire*; above, Introduction.
90 HRO, 65M72/PZ1.
91 Above, Social History.
92 *Doing the Duty*, 37–8.
93 HRO, 21M65/E2/249; 21M65/E7/9/100, 115, 130.
94 HRO, 21M65/B1/154.
95 HRO, 35M48/6/1467; *Alumni Oxon*. I, 8; HRO, 24M49/22; 21M65/E2/250.
96 HRO, 21M65/E6/9.

While criticism may well have been justified, the work of diligent curates has perhaps been overlooked in assessing the state of the church at this time, and the Dummer statistics suggest this to have been the case. Two services with sermons were held each Sunday in the early 1800s, with eight confirmations in 1821, 21 in 1831 and nine in 1835. An annual average of over 11 baptisms, seven burials and two marriages was recorded in the ten years from 1821.[97] Sixty children attended Sunday school in 1821. By 1851 average attendance at the Sunday morning service was 150, with 130 at the afternoon service (the recorded population of the parish in that year was 409).[98] Stephen Terry provides a portrait of church life in his diary entry for 24 March 1847 thus:

> The General Fast Day. I never before was at Dummer church so well attended – all our own parishioners and all devoutly disposed, or appeared to be so, to implore from the almighty pardon for the remission of their sins, as well as feeling deeply for the suffering and destruction of our miserable Irish neighbours. Stephen [his son] gave us an admirable sermon. The service was so long that we had no sermon in the afternoon.[99]

Sir William Dunbar (Magdalen Hall, Oxford) had been minister of the Floating Church and chaplain to the Sailors' Home while holding curacies in London and then serving as rector of Walwyn Castle, Haverford West (Pembs.), before coming to Dummer in 1875.[100] Some indication of his beliefs and outlook may be obtained from a codicil to his will (1881) in which he bequeathed to his son three gold studs bearing the initials of friends and containing pieces of their hair, who represented for him the characteristics of conscientiousness, courage and catholicity.[101] The three were: James Blair Oliphant, 10th laird of Gask in Perthshire, Revd Edward Irving, a Scottish minister who inspired a movement known as the Catholic Apostolic Church,[102] and Revd Edward Bickersteth, an evangelical clergyman and secretary of the Church Missionary Society.[103]

In 1898 the parish was served by the rector, George Jones, churchwardens Sir Richard Rycroft and James Billimore of Clump House and lay help including three district visitors and four Sunday school teachers. Both the organist and choir were paid. There was an average attendance at Sunday services of 70 in the mornings and 100 – including 30 Sunday school children – in the afternoons, with 25 on weekdays. Communion was administered once a month at 8.30am and once at midday, a pattern suggesting a 'low' churchmanship.[104] A new organ by Charles Martin of Oxford, costing £150, had been installed in memory of Sir Richard Rycroft's brother.[105] Among other gifts to the church, the Rycroft family gave a reredos, three pictures in a frame – *The Annunciation* by Botticelli and at the sides St Michael and St George – in memory of

---

97   HRO, 21M65/B5/2.
98   *Rel. Census*, 187; *Census*, 1851.
99   HRO, 24M49/1–22.
100 *Winton Dioc. Cal.*, 1877, 146.
101 HRO, 5M62, 397.
102 *ODNB*, s.v. Irving, Edward (d. 1834), Scottish minister (accessed 3 Oct. 2017).
103 *ODNB*, s.v. Bickersteth, Edward (d. 1850), Church of England clergyman and evangelical leader (accessed 3 Oct. 2017).
104 HRO, 21M65/B4/5.
105 Ibid.; plaque on organ.

Lady Rycroft (d. 1917).[106] The central east window was given by Canon Blunt and family in 1892, and installed when the east wall was rebuilt under the supervision of J.P. St Aubyn.[107] Two Kempe windows were also given by Canon Blunt, then of Burghclere rectory, and his niece in 1913. They commemorate Shirley Anna Blunt (d. 1900) and John Lawrell, priest, who ministered in the church 1839–41.[108]

1900–2020

When surveyed at the beginning of the 20th century, the nave was in poor condition, with remedial work being carried out in 1911.[109] During the First World War there were 60 communicants on the roll and an average of 40 children in the Sunday school; church organisations were active including the Girls Friendly Society, Mothers' Union and a mothers' meeting.[110] The parish lost 13 men during the war including Llewellyn Jones, the youngest son of the rector who had died of his wounds in France in 1916.[111] The church, said to be for 110 in 1905, saw 180 people 'packed in' on 1 November 1919 when the war memorial lychgate was dedicated.[112] George Jones resigned in 1925 after 43 years in the parish.[113]

Another long-serving incumbent, Arthur Ireland, a graduate of Trinity College, Dublin, was rector from 1926 to 1959, the last to serve the single parish.[114] During Ireland's service a parochial church council was established, meeting quarterly. In 1931, 19 male and 17 female parishioners were confirmed and in 1936 average congregations were reported as 30–40 on Sunday mornings and 40–50 in the evening. Ireland was less than complimentary about the Methodist chapel's programme of brass bands, concert parties and other 'attractions' of the sort, questioning the religious value of such methods and claiming that there was plenty of room for 'cheerfulness' in the services of the church.[115]

In 1962, after a vacancy, William Basil Norris MA was appointed rector of North Waltham, Steventon and Dummer.[116] From 1968 he was assisted by the Venerable Richard Rudgard OBE, emeritus archdeacon of Basingstoke and chaplain to the Queen, as curate-in-charge of Dummer.[117] Richard Rudgard became rector of the new benefice of Ellisfield, Farleigh Wallop and Dummer in 1972.[118] Cliddesden was added to the benefice in 1983 and the four parishes joined together (as Farleigh benefice) within the united benefice of Farleigh, Candover and Wield created in 2010; Stephen Mourant BTh

106 HRO, 21M65/114F/4. The reredos, evident in a photograph of 2008 (church leaflet), was displayed in the gallery in 2018.
107 Pevsner, *North Hampshire*, 239; *VCH Hants*. III, 359.
108 HRO, 21M65/114F/1,114F/2.
109 *VCH Hants*. III, 359; HRO, 65M72/PV1 (Tie rod across east end as side walls giving way, 1911).
110 HRO, 21M65/B/6/6.
111 HRO, TOP94/1/1.
112 HRO, 110M98/1.
113 HRO, 35M48/6/3006.
114 Ibid.
115 HRO, 21M65/B4/10.
116 HRO, 35M48/6A/2/15.
117 *Crockford's Clerical Dir.*, 1997–9, 883–4.
118 Ibid., 884.

was associate rector, holding special responsibility for them.[119] The pattern of services, rotating between the churches with one service at Dummer on each of four Sundays in a month and with joint services held on occasion, was disrupted by the restrictions imposed in 2020 to combat the coronavirus pandemic. Online services were introduced during the time of church closures.[120]

Lay involvement was exemplified by churchwarden Lieutenant Colonel Peter Clifton (1911–96), who is commemorated in the glass of the south window in the nave, installed in 1997. Another churchwarden, Colonel Andrew Ferguson, arranged for a regimental standard of the Life Guards to be laid up in the church.[121] Fundraising to restore and re-hang the bells with modern bearings in 2011 provided a good example of parishioners coming together in support of the church.[122]

The Church of All Saints

All Saints' church and churchyard stand on slightly raised ground on the side of the road leading to Farleigh and near the junction of Up Street and Down Street. Its village setting adds to its charm and its position is such that in 1881 it was said that no house lay more than one mile from the church.[123] The former rectory lies on the other side of the Farleigh road in its own grounds. The church comprises a single-bay nave with a small chancel, west porch and bell turret. The earliest surviving fabric is from the 12th century and has escaped over-zealous restoration, being subject instead to piecemeal repairs. The church is built of flint with some brick in-filling, buttressing and bracing. The steep pitched roofs of nave and chancel are tiled.

The earliest surviving fabric, perhaps from the 12th century, consists of a plain round-headed doorway in the south wall of the nave, blocked up and now a window, and has probable Norman masonry.[124] A more definite dating of c.1200 has been given to the chancel arch and to the chancel itself.[125] There is a small priest's doorway on the north side of the chancel which is lit by three lancets on each side and a group of three which form the east window. The short nave (12 m.) is comparatively broad (6.2 m.) and is well-lit by large three-light Perpendicular windows on both the south and north walls, one fragment of coloured glass revealing their former state. On the north wall of the nave is a low moulded segmental arch of a 14th-century tomb recess. In the early 20th century, a Purbeck marble tomb slab was visible but the recess has since been infilled, perhaps to reinforce the nave wall.[126] On the northern side of the chancel arch is a large, empty image niche, or space for the reredos of a lay altar.[127]

---

119 *Crockford's Clerical Dir.*, 2016–17, 159, 630.
120 *Hill and Dale,* monthly editions.
121 HRO, 21M65/114F/9.
122 Napier, *Dummer Bells.*
123 HRO, 10557/SP374.
124 Pevsner, *North Hampshire,* 239.
125 NHLE, no. 1093019, Ch. of All Saints (accessed 18 Mar. 2018); Pevsner, *North Hampshire,* 239.
126 *VCH Hants.* III, 359.
127 NHLE, no. 1093019, Ch. of All Saints (accessed 18 Mar. 2018).

In the west porch above the inner door is an empty image niche, another example of iconoclasm in the church which occurred either at the beginning of the Reformation or during the Civil Wars when troops besieging nearby Basing House did much damage to religious buildings in the area. Of a similar age and on either side of the chancel arch are squints. On the northern side the sightline to the altar was blocked when an organ was installed but on the other side is a round-headed squint which was opened up and restored in 2000.[128]

The west door opens into the church beneath a low gallery that extends nearly half-way up the nave, leaving the western end of the nave with a low ceiling. Huge oak posts support the gallery and form the basis for the bell turret. The square turret inserted in the nave roof in the early or mid 15th century has weather-boarded sides and wooden louvres with a pyramid slate roof. It is similar to others in the area of a like age, Mapledurwell, Silchester and Old Burghclere being good examples. The medieval timber-framing of the roof and belfry are considered to be among the earliest and best preserved of their respective types in north Hampshire.[129]

The 15th-century porch has two small lancet windows and a range of carvings – geometrical designs, initials and figures – on the door pillars and around the windows.

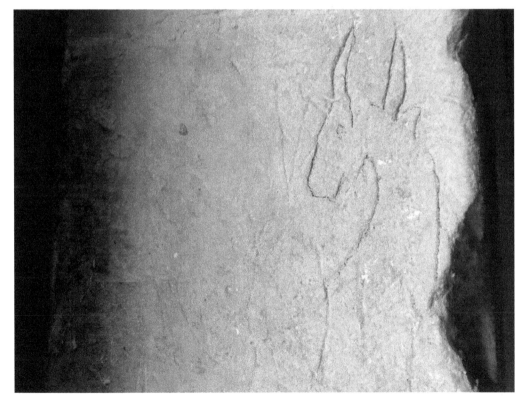

Figure 35 *Horned head graffiti, possibly an ox head or a crested helm, on north side of porch doorway.*

---

128 Pevsner, *North Hampshire*, 239.
129 R. Warmington, RIBA, survey for NHLE, Nov. 1979.

These were surveyed by the Hampshire Field Club in 2017 and are thought to be medieval graffiti, similar to those in St Michael's church, Basingstoke, and elsewhere in Hampshire.[130]

Narrow stairs inside the west doorway lead to the ringing chamber and through it to the gallery. The gallery dates from *c*.1660–85,[131] during the incumbency of Hugh Davis, and a coat of arms of Charles II, inscribed 1672, may have been installed in the church at the same time, reflecting his loyalty to the Crown. On the wall of the belfry are 'Rules for Ringers', written in the 17th century, only partially decipherable in 2020. There are five bells, three given by John Millingate between 1590 and 1599 and cast by Joseph Carter of Reading, one cast in 1759 by Thomas Swain of Co. Longford, re-cast by the Whitechapel foundry in 1911, and the treble cast in 1811 by James Wells of Aldbourne.[132] A sanctus bell hangs outside the belfry.

Among the furniture and fittings of special note are a small carved wood pulpit constructed *c*.1380 and above the chancel arch and tie beam a rare example of a 15th-century curved timber rood canopy.[133] Its vibrant blue paint and gold bosses are indicative of the colour that would have been found elsewhere in the pre-reformation church. The communion rails are late 17th century, notable for their strong twisted balusters. Brasses include a palimpsest to Robert Clark *c*.1500, with reused inscription to Allys Magewick (d. 1591) and a slab with the brass figures of William at Moore *alias* Dommer (d. 1593), kneeling at a desk. The figure of his wife, Katherine (Brydges), noted in the early 20th century is now lost and that of their son, kneeling behind his father, has lost its head.[134] The accompanying inscription in the east wall of the chancel has details of his life and beneath this his grave slab:

> I William at moore Dommer calde, doe here entoumbed lye
> And Lordship this and of thys churche, the patronage had I.
> Myne Ancestors me longe before, weare owners of the same
> Obtaynd by matche with Dommers heire wherof they tooke ye name
> Which name and living here on earthe as from them I possesse
> Soe now on earthe like them I am for wormes become a gueste.
> Thus (reader) deathe on me hath wrought that to mankind is due
> And like of thee by natures course, is sure for to ensue.

The east wall was rebuilt in flint in 1893 under the supervision of J.P. St Aubyn, apparently in connection with the installation of the three lancet east windows.[135] The glass in these windows is by C.E. Kempe & Co. and is contemporary with those in St Leonard's church in neighbouring Cliddesden, also by Kempe.[136] The central window represents the Crucifixion. John the Baptist and St Cecilia are depicted in windows, also by Kempe, on the south and north walls of the chancel respectively.[137] Prescription

---

130 www.Hantsfieldclub.org.uk/medieval-graffiti/completed/dummer-all-saints.html (accessed 11 Apr. 2018).
131 Pevsner, *North Hampshire*, 240.
132 Napier, *Dummer Bells*, unpag.; *VCH Hants*. III, 359.
133 NHLE, no. 1093019, Ch. of All Saints (accessed 18 Mar. 2018); Pevsner, *North Hampshire*, 239.
134 *Hants*. III, 359; Pevsner, *North Hampshire*, 240.
135 HRO, 21M65114F/1.
136 *Cliddesden, Hatch and Farleigh Wallop*, 76.
137 HRO, 21565/114F/2.

Figure 36 *All Saints' church, pulpit constructed c.1380.*

Figure 37 *All Saints' church showing c.15th-century rood canopy over the chancel arch.*

panels and paintings of the Ten Commandments hang high on the walls on either side of the chancel arch. The octagonal stone font is Victorian and stands in a recess near the west door. A painted donation board recording charitable gifts to the parish hangs on the north wall and not far from it is a large memorial to members of the Terry family. Repairs to the nave included a tie rod, added in 1911, across the east end because the side walls were giving way. The south wall was rendered in the 20th century which may have obscured other repairs.[138] The church was re-seated in 1923 – the work undertaken by local carpenter F. Smith – the cost of £210 defrayed by public subscriptions.[139] The bells were restored and re-hung in 2011 at a cost of £35,000 and the small window on the south wall of the porch was re-glazed to commemorate this work.[140]

The churchyard is walled on two sides and was closed to burials in 1856. A cemetery was opened at the same time, close-by in Up Street, and in 2020 remained under the auspices of the parochial church council. The churchyard contains 18th- and early 19th-century tombstones, many of the inscriptions illegible, and several cast metal tombstones, perhaps made in the village foundry. A large cross close to the west door commemorates Edward Walter Blunt (1779–1860) of Kempshott House and members

138 HRO, 65M72/PV1.
139 HRO, 21M65/114F/5.
140 Napier, *Dummer Bells*, 33.

Figure 38 *The lychgate erected in 1919 as a war memorial.*

of the family. It fell in the great storm of 1987 and was re-erected in 2006.[141] In 2020 the grounds were cared for by villagers, working by rota.

Lady Rycroft, wife of Sir Richard, designed the lychgate based on that of a porch at Boxford church, Suffolk. The lychgate used timbers from an ancient barn at Dummer Grange.[142] The names of 13 men from the parish who gave their lives in the First World War and of five men who fell in the Second World War are inscribed on the outer side.

Methodism

John Wesley preached twice in the parish, in 1736 and 1739, but evidence of firmly rooted Methodism only dates from the early 19th century. In 1828 a licence was granted for the house of Joseph Woolridge, a labourer, to be used for religious worship; John Overton of Andover was the minister.[143] In the same year a licence was granted for the house of James Barber to be used by Wesleyan Methodists.[144] Between 1833 and 1841 a further

141 www.asdguide.btck.co.uk (accessed 23 July 2017).
142 Ibid.; HRO, 65M72/PZ3; 41M64/PZ15.
143 HRO, 21M65/F2/4/310.
144 HRO, 21M65/F2/4/324.

Figure 39 *The former Primitive Methodist chapel, Down Street.*

three licences were granted.[145] In 1841 Stephen Terry, lord of the manor, took steps to prevent 'ranters' – a pejorative name given to Primitive Methodists – from assembling on waste ground in the village.[146] Despite the early Wesleyan links Dummer became part of the Micheldever Primitive Methodist circuit. By 1851 the Basingstoke circuit had been formed from Micheldever and the Dummer society had 16 full members with 15 on trial. In 1861 Thomas Alderslade, a bricklayer, was recorded as a Primitive Methodist preacher[147] and the following year, 1862, a Primitive Methodist chapel was built in Down Street.[148] The purpose for which the land was required had been kept hidden during the sale for fear that, if known, the transaction might not have been agreed, an indication of the attitude of landowners to what was clearly regarded as a challenge to the established church.[149] Numbers attending the chapel were such that in 1867 an extension was added.[150] Like a number of chapels in the Basingstoke circuit, land purchase, building costs of £140 and maintenance costs left a debt and efforts were made through collections and fundraising to clear this.[151] Renovations to the chapel were carried out in 1891.[152] Not more than eight

145 HRO, 21M65/F2/5/99, 235; F2/6/29.
146 HRO, 24M49/1, 19 Oct. 1841.
147 www.myprimitivemethodists.org.uk (accessed 15 Jan. 2018); *Census*, 1861.
148 HRO, 57M77/NMC5.
149 www.myprimitivemethodists.org.uk (accessed 15 Jan. 2018).
150 HRO, 57M77/NMC6, June 1867.
151 HRO, 57M77/NMS14.
152 HRO, 57M77/NMC8.

to ten people were said to usually attend the Primitive Methodist chapel services in 1898, although this could have been an underestimate.[153]

From the early days of Primitive Methodism in Dummer, 'Camp Meetings' – outdoor preaching – had been part of their programme of evangelism.[154] Such meetings occurred once a year in the summers of 1906, 1907 and occasionally until the 1920s, and a week's mission was planned in 1910.[155] Financial solvency was the other continual concern. Dummer was one of the poorest chapels in the Basingstoke circuit and developments at Cliddesden and Farleigh Wallop were discouraged by the circuit officers in order for resources to be concentrated in the one centre.[156] Fundraising was therefore important and social events played an important part in this.[157] In 1914 a gift of a new stove, piping and general repairs carried out by Bro. R. Wyeth of Oakley was warmly acknowledged by the circuit. Members of the Cliddesden Wesleyan chapel walked to Dummer on Easter Monday, 1923, for a tea and evening concert, illustrating friendly links ahead of the formal joining of the two branches in the Methodist Church in 1932.[158] The local society's records are limited but by the 1950s support for the chapel appears to have waned despite the efforts of a few stalwarts.[159] Mr F. Chivers was named for his work with the Sunday school in 1927 and in 1932, when 50 children were on the roll, and in 1943 Mrs Brazier of Box Cottage was recognised for her Sunday school teaching.[160] Mrs Wake and her children also feature in the records as strong supporters of chapel life. However, by 1960 numbers were such that the chapel could not continue and it closed in 1964. The premises were sold for commercial purposes and proceeds of the sale were diverted to a new building scheme in South Ham, Basingstoke.[161]

153 HRO, 21M65/B4/5.
154 HRO, 57M77/NMC6. Examples in June 1865, Jul. 1866, June 1867.
155 HRO, 57M77/NMC10.
156 HRO, 57M/77/NMC9, Sept. 1898.
157 HRO, 57M77/NMS14. Examples: 1931: male voice choir, brass band concert in village hall.
158 *Hants. and Berks. Gaz.*, 14 Apr. 1923.
159 HRO, 57M77/NMS14. The account book had pages torn out of it before it was deposited in HRO.
160 *Hants. and Berks. Gaz.*, 9 Sept. 1932; HRO, 57M77/NMC11, 12.
161 HRO, 57M77/NMS99.

Manorial Court Records

The manor was for centuries the main unit of local government, and the court rolls, which contain the accounts of the manorial court proceedings, are a valuable source of written local records before the mid 16th century. They are therefore of great importance for the parish historian, who is fortunate indeed if court rolls survive for his/her area of study. The earliest extant roll in England dates from 1246 but by the 1270s such documents were plentiful. The courts continued throughout parts of the country into the 18th century and are a major source of evidence on medieval communities and the life and work of manorial tenants.

The lord of a manor had the right to hold a court for his local tenants; known as the court baron, this was usually held every three weeks. It is possible to follow the names of the families, freemen or villeins who appear in these records, sometimes for many generations. The records also show who held what land and on what terms. Thus new tenants came to the court to swear fealty to the lord and to meet the customary fines and fees of the manor, usually in the form of a heriot, best horse or cow, and a relief, a monetary payment.

> The Homage present that William Soper free tenant of this Manor is dead since the last court and that there happened to the Lord by his death an Heriot, viz. the best animal which was a cow of the value of 25s. and were paid to the Lord, and a Relief viz. 1s. which is not yet paid and that William, the son of the said William is the heir of the said William deceased.
>
> Manor of West Dummer, 23 March 1667/8

The system of copyhold tenure originates in these courts, as villeins had their title to land written in the court roll of which they held a copy. Labour services, including regular weekly work on the lord's demesne, were in time commuted to a monetary

Figure 40 *Farmer with wife and two cows, ploughing a field, 14th century.*

rent, although various seasonal services such as haymaking, reaping, ploughing in Lent and winter and carting wood might be required of a villein. As late as 1692 in Dummer, two days reaping in the field was included in a tenancy agreement.

The agricultural routine of the manor was regulated by the courts. Where an open field system operated, an active landowner, the lord of the manor, gave detailed orders for the management of the fields and for grazing on common pastures. These included matters such as the date that hedges should be cut, crops sown, land left fallow, animals let onto commons, the 'stints' – numbers of animals allowed at any time and suchlike. Fines were imposed for offenders against the regime, the size of such payments indicating the seriousness in which the offence was regarded. The resulting information provides an invaluable picture and understanding of farming before enclosure of the land took place from the 17th century onwards. Field names, landscape features, the church calendar – by which dates were measured – all add to the knowledge that may be gained from these records.

> the court ordered that every person for his part shall sufficiently make the hedges about the common barley fields yearly sown before the feast of St George … default 6s. 8d.
>
> the court ordered that no man shall take any beast to be or go in any of the commons of this manor but that he and they shall first give knowledge and warning to the haywards of the manor for the time being … default 5s.
>
> the court ordered that no person do suffer his hogs or pigs to go or be out of their several gates at any time of the year not being ringed or pegged. And that any person do keep his hogs and pigs from henceforth in his several gates or several grounds from the first day of Pentecost yearly until the fields shall be full rid and the corn carried out of the same fields … default 6s. 8d.
>
> Manor of East Dummer, 6 June 1598

The court also dealt with disputes between individuals, the recovery of small debts and complaints of trespass. However, details of more serious offences may be found in the records of courts known as courts leet, usually held every six months either by the lord of the manor or sometimes as part of the hundred court. As well as cases of common nuisance and affrays, frequent entries may be found of the names of persons, often women, who had broken the laws regarding the price and quality of bread and ale. This can be seen as a form of licensing; nevertheless, excessive prices or the selling of bad food was punished.

Officially up until 1733, apart from the period of the Commonwealth, court rolls were written in Latin, although the actual proceedings were conducted in English. Some records contain a mixture of both Latin and English and a number in the 16th and 17th century are fully in English. As well as the records of courts baron and courts leet, the court of survey held by a new lord contained details of all landholdings in the manor and is another valuable research tool. It should be remembered that sometimes the manor coincided with the parish boundaries but that sometimes there was more than one manor within a parish.

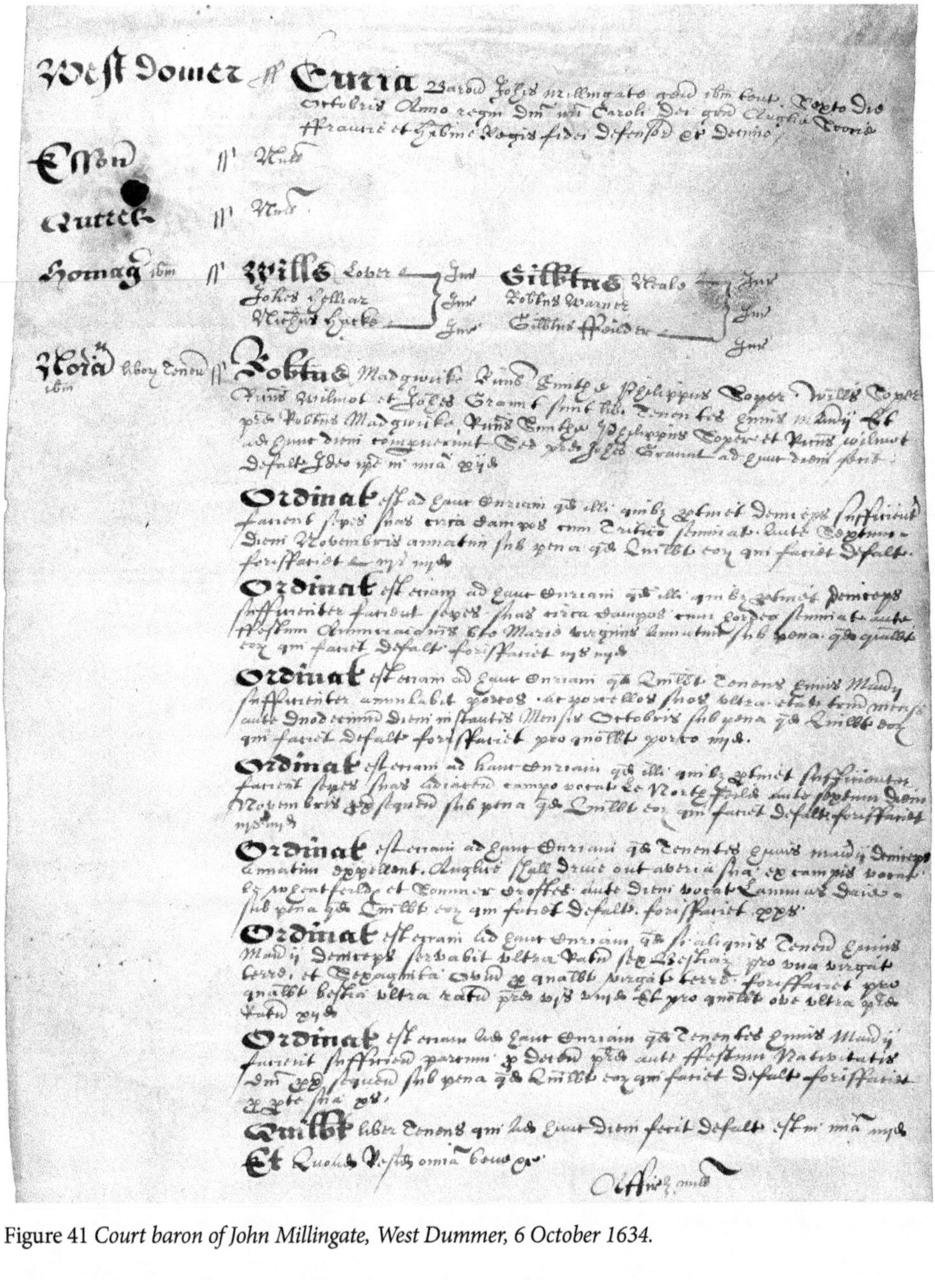

Figure 41 *Court baron of John Millingate, West Dummer, 6 October 1634.*

LOCAL GOVERNMENT

IN THE MIDDLE AGES DUMMER was governed through the manorial courts of East and West Dummer and the hundred court of Bermondspit which met in Nutley. Dummer formed part of the lower tithing of Bermondspit hundred, the hundreds being subdivisions of the county which had their own courts and officers. Locally chosen tithingmen reported infringements of the peace and administered taxation demands. This was a role filled by prominent men in the community such as Richard Penton, a tithingman in the 17th century who was a free tenant with land in both East and West Dummer.[1] All persons between 12 and 70 years of age were required to attend the court, with specific notifications issued by the overseers of the poor and the churchwardens to those charged with offences.[2] In September 1673 the tithingmen of Dummer were summoned to a courts leet or sheriff's tourn by the steward of the Bermondspit court with demands for a year's 'Lady' or 'Law day' money of 5s. 1d., payable by 15 tenants, and for payment of vicontiel money, a tax collected for the crown.[3] Kempshott, by contrast, lay in Basingstoke hundred and the tithingman was expected to report to its court.

Manorial Government

A series of court rolls from the manors of East and West Dummer survive from the period 1537–1729, most of which appear to be courts baron.[4] The earliest of the 34 rolls is for a court held in 1537 by William Dummer, lord of West Dummer.[5] Even after the manors came into common ownership separate courts were held, although they frequently took place on the same day and were presided over by a shared steward. The courts appointed officers including haywards whose duties were stated in 1688 'to look to the common hedges ... and to the corn and fetch the beasts at evenings'. John Redding, William Bye and William Lover were named as the lord's haywards in 1615 and were empowered to impound the cattle of any person breaking the court's orders. To encourage the haywards in their duties they were allowed to retain one third of the fees paid for the cattle to be released.[6] Other positions such as supervisors of the sheep and cattle on the commons were required to ensure that numbers of animals did not exceed that agreed and the holders were rewarded by receiving the fine of 6d. for each animal over the limit, with

---

1   HRO, 44M69/G3/145/29; 55M67/M14.
2   HRO, 55M67/M2; 44M69/G3/145/2; 44M69/G3/145/29.
3   HRO, 55M67/M2. Lady money may refer to Lady Day 25 March, a quarter day.
4   HRO, 55M67/M3–M37.
5   HRO, 55M67/M30.
6   HRO, 55M67/M16.

6d. also paid to the lord.[7] Affeerers (assessors) decided the value of fines for various infringements. In 1609 it was agreed Walter Madgwicke and John Cooper should assess and allot how much every tenant of East Dummer should pay towards the making of a common gate called Salt Gate, a sum to be paid promptly with a penalty for refusal of 3s. 8d; co-operation within the manor was essential for its way of life.[8]

Co-operation also existed between the manorial lords. In 1554 William Dummer, lord of West Dummer, with the consent of William Dale, lord of East Dummer, agreed the numbers of animals to be pastured on a yardland[9] (the stint), and in 1583 William Dummer and John Millingate, lord of East Dummer, agreed orders to be kept 'for the common weal, quietness and profit of the tenants and inhabitants of the said parish'.[10] The same court ordered that the three farmers of the parish should contribute towards a national tax called the 'fifteenths'. Presumably this referred to the demesne farms of the three manors. In 1666 the tenants of all three manors within the parish were ordered 'to meet at the walnut tree by the church on Tuesday in Rogation week to set out the bounds in difference between party and party'.[11] No court records have been found for the Grange. Its inhabitants may have become subject to the West Dummer court once the two manors were in common ownership; prior to this the Grange, as part of the Waverley Abbey estates, may have been exempted by episcopal authority from civil action.[12] Although the manors were managed as separate units there was also a sense of a parish identity, maintaining parish boundaries and not letting land or grazing rights to 'strangers' from outside the parish.[13]

Parochial Government

Churchwardens and overseers of the poor played an increasingly important role in parish government from the 16th century onwards and churchwardens' accounts survive for Dummer from 1731. What was known as the 'parish vestry' – meetings held in the church vestry (where there was one) and chaired by the rector – dealt with the administration of poor relief, maintenance of highways and other secular affairs as well as church business. Churchwardens' accounts illustrate the extent of their responsibilities from paying for ditching at Salt Gate in 1731 and mending the Down Gate in 1736.[14] Other duties included several purchases of sparrows at 3d. or 6d. a dozen and 4d. paid for a polecat – all in attempts to control vermin under the Elizabethan vermin laws – while the entries for three seamen in 1731 and 12 vagrants in 1740 indicate their responsibility for destitute travellers.[15] The vestry minutes of 1886 record the appointments of Mr P. Budd and Mr R. Edward Cobden as overseers for the coming year and Mr M. Batting

7   HRO, 55M67/M11.
8   HRO, 55M67/M8.
9   HRO, 55M67/M34.
10 HRO, 55M67/M35.
11 HRO, 55M67/M15.
12 VCH Surr. II, 80.
13 HRO, 55M67/M11, M15, M29.
14 HRO, 65M72/PZ1.
15 Above, Social History.

as guardian.[16] Poor relief had been removed from parish responsibilities after 1834 with the establishment of poor law unions, so the only extant account books of the overseers for the period of 1922–7 are of more limited interest, payments being made to the union rather than to individuals.[17]

Dummer with Kempshott civil parish was established under the Local Government Act of 1894. As part of the Act's aim to democratise local government, five parish councillors were elected in that year: Charles Butt (58) carpenter, Tower Hill Cottage, Thomas Chivers (43) farm labourer, Down Lane, H. Complin, William John Cooper (43) farmer, Grange Farm House and Robert Lockwood (43) retired army captain, Dummer House.[18] In 1913 the five parish councillors were: Montague Billimore (46) florist, Clump House, Thomas Chivers (60) hedger, Dummer, George Page (61) master blacksmith, Dummer, Revd George Jones (69) rector, Sir Richard Rycroft (51) Major, Hants. Carabiniers, Dummer House.[19] On both occasions those elected included a spread of occupations and social status, offering a wide representation of the community, something that had been hoped for in the creation of this new style of parish government. The parish was within Basingstoke Rural District Council in 1894 and with local government reorganisation in 1974 became part of Basingstoke and Deane District Council.

During the 20th century the work of the council involved planning and environmental issues as well as the development of leisure facilities. Concerns included telephone and postal facilities, bus services, tree preservation, the problems caused by increasing motor traffic through the village and the impact of the M3 motorway slicing through the north of the parish.[20] The parish was renamed 'Dummer CP' in 1989 to reflect the transfer of land in Kempshott to Basingstoke borough that had occurred in 1985.[21]

In 2020 the parish council consisted of only five members and a clerk despite the wide fluctuations in population that had occurred since 2000. As well as reporting to an annual parish assembly, quarterly newsletters kept parishioners well informed of the council's activities. While responsibility for the Beggarwood ward was transferred to Basingstoke in May 2003, a major consideration related to other housing developments north of the motorway and whether the boundary between the parish and the borough of Basingstoke should be redrawn to reflect the realities of the urban/rural divide.[22]

16   HRO, 65M72 /PZ1.
17   HRO, 68M72/DU20.
18   *Hants. and Berks. Gaz.*, 8 Dec. 1894; *Census*, 1891.
19   *Hants. and Berks. Gaz.*, 22 Mar. 1913; *Census*, 1911; *Hants. Year Book*, 1912.
20   Parish Council Minutes, unpubl.
21   Basingstoke and Deane Dist. Council, *Parish Name Change,* 27 July 1989; Basingstoke and Deane (Parishes) Order, 1985; HRO, H/CS6/1/6/5.
22   J. Jones, *Annual Parish Newsletters,* 2003–17.

ABBREVIATIONS

a.	acre(s)
Abbrev. Rot. Orig.	*Rotulorum Originalium Abbreviatio, temp. Hen. III, Edw. I* (Record Commission, 1805)
Ad.	*Advertiser*
Alumni Oxon.	J. Foster (ed.), *Alumni Oxonienses 1500–1714* (4 vols, Oxford, 1891–2); *1715–1886* (4 vols, Oxford, 1887–8)
Austen, *Letters*	D. Le Faye (ed.), *Jane Austen's Letters* (3rd edn, Oxford, 1995)
Baigent and Millard, *Basingstoke*	F.J. Baigent and J.E. Millard, *A History of the Ancient Town and Manor of Basingstoke in the County of Southampton*, 2 vols (Basingstoke, 1889)
BDBC	Basingstoke and Deane Borough Council
BHAS	Basingstoke Historical and Archaeological Society
Bingley, *Hampshire*	HRO, 16M79/15: William Bingley, *History of Hampshire Parishes*
BL	British Library
BTH	Basingstoke Talking History
Bond, Pendomer	T. Bond, 'Pendomer in co. Somerset', *Proc. Somerset Archaeological and Natural Hist. Soc.* 17 (1871), 91–115
Calamy Revised	A.G. Matthews, *Being a Revision of Edmund Calamy's* 'Account of the ministers and others ejected and silenced, 1660–2' (Oxford, 1934)
Cal. Close	*Calendar of the Close Rolls preserved in the Public Record Office* (HMSO, 1892–1963)
Cal. Inq. p.m.	*Calendar of Inquisitions post mortem, preserved in the Public Record Office* (HMSO, 1904–2009)
Cal. Inq. p.m. Hen. VII	*Calendar of Inquisitions post mortem, Henry VII* (HMSO, 1898–1955)
Cal. Pat.	*Calendar of the Patent Rolls preserved in the Public Record Office* (HMSO, 1891–1986)

Cal. SP Dom.	*Calendar of State Papers, Domestic Series* (HMSO, 1856–2006)
Cat. Anct. Deeds	*A Descriptive Catalogue of Ancient Deeds in the Public Record Office* (HMSO, 1890–1915)
Chambers, *Machine Breakers*	J. Chambers, *Hampshire Machine Breakers: The Story of the 1830 Riots* (Letchworth, 1996)
Chapman and Seeliger, *Enclosure in Hampshire*	J. Chapman and S. Seeliger, *A Guide to Enclosure in Hampshire 1700–1900*, HCC (Winchester, 1997)
Char. Com.	Charity Commission
Charities Report	*Commissioners of Inquiry into Charities in England and Wales: 14th Report* (Parl. Papers 1826 (382))
Cliddesden, Hatch and Farleigh Wallop	A. Deveson and S. Lane, *Cliddesden, Hatch and Farleigh Wallop* (The Victoria History of Hampshire, 2018)
Compton Census	A. Whiteman (ed.), *The Compton Census of 1676: A Critical Edition* (Records of Social and Economic History, n.s. 10, London, 1986)
Conservation Area	BDBC, *Dummer Conservation Area Appraisal* (Basingstoke, 1981)
Council on Education	*Committee of Council on Education* (Parl. Papers 1883 [C.3706–1])
CP	Civil Parish
Crockford's Clerical Dir.	*Crockford's Clerical Directory*
Design Statement	BDBC, *Dummer Village Design Statement* (Basingstoke, 2004)
Dioc. Pop. Returns	A. Dyer and D.M. Palliser (eds), *The Diocesan Population Returns for 1563 and 1603* (Records of Social and Economic History, n.s. 31, Oxford, 2005)
Dir.	*Directory*
Doing the Duty	M. Smith (ed.), *Doing the Duty of the Parish: Surveys of the Church in Hampshire, 1810* (HRS 17, 2004)
Domesday	A. Williams and G.H. Martin (eds.), *Domesday Book: a Complete Translation* (London, 2002)
Educ. Enquiry Abstract	*Education Enquiry: Abstract of the Answers and Returns* (Parl. Papers 1835 (62) i)
Educ. of Poor Digest	*Digest of Parochial Returns on the Education of the Poor* (Parl. Papers 1818 (224) ii)

Ekwall, *English Place-Names*	E. Ekwall, *The Concise Oxford Dictionary of English Place-Names* (Oxford, 1951)
Endowed Charities, 1873, 1898	*Digest of Endowed Charities (County of Southampton)* (Parl. Papers 1873 (25-4), 1898 (131))
Excerpta e Rot. Finium	*Excerpta e Rotulis Finium*, Hen. III, 2 vols (Rec. Com., 1835-6)
f. (ff.)	folio(s)
Feudal Aids	*Inquisitions and Assessments relating to Feudal Aids preserved in the Public Record Office*, 6 vols (HMSO, 1899-1920)
Gaz.	Gazette
Glasscock (ed.), *Subsidy*	R.E. Glasscock (ed.), *The Lay Subsidy of 1334 1334* (British Academy Records of Social and Economic Hist. n.s. 2, 1975)
Golding, *Kempshot Manor*	C.D.L. Golding, *The Manor of Kempshot Hampshire Seat of George IV [Prince Regent] as Prince of Wales c.1788 to 1795* (unpubl. dissertation, University of Portsmouth, 1992)
ha.	hectare(s)
Hants. Ad.	*Hampshire Advertiser*
Hants. Chron.	*Hampshire Chronicle*
Hants. Lay Subsidy 1586	C.R. Davey (ed.), *The Hampshire Lay Subsidy Rolls, 1586* (HRS 4, 1981)
Hants. Tax List 1327	P. Mitchell-Fox and M. Page (eds), *The Hampshire Tax List of 1327* (HRS 20, 2014)
Hants. HER	Hampshire Historic Environment Record, https://www.Hants.gov.uk
HCC	Hampshire County Council
Hearth Tax 1665	E. Hughes and P. White (eds), *The Hampshire Hearth Tax Assessment, 1665* (HRS 11, 1991)
Hill and Dale	*Hill and Dale, A Farleigh Parish Review*, monthly editions
Hist. Parl.	*The History of Parliament: Commons* (1964–2022, in progress): accessed online at www.historyofparliamentonline.org
HRO	Hampshire Record Office
HRS	Hampshire Record Series
HRSoc.	Hampshire Record Society
Kelly's Dir. Hants.	*Kelly's Directory of Hampshire and the Isle of Wight*

LGBO	Local Government Boundary Order
LPL	Lambeth Palace Library
L&P Hen. VIII	*Letters and Papers, Foreign and Domestic, of the Reign of Henry VIII* (HMSO, 1864-1932)
Mapledurwell	J. Hare, J. Morrin and S. Waight, *Mapledurwell* (The Victoria History of Hampshire, 2012)
Napier, *Kempshott Park*	S. Napier, *Burning Passions – A Brief History of Kempshott Park* (unpubl. monograph, 2015)
n.d.	no date
NHLE	National Heritage List for England, https://historicengland.org.uk/listing/the-list/
Nonarum Inquisitiones	*Nonarum Inquisitiones in Curia Scaccarii* (Rec. Com., 1807)
n.s.	new series
ODNB	Oxford Dictionary of National Biography (Oxford, 2004); www.oxforddnb.com
OS	Ordnance Survey
Parl. Writs	F. Palgrave (ed.) *The Parliamentary writs and writs of military summons, together with the records and muniments relating to the suit and service due and performed to the King's high court of Parliament and the councils of the realm or affording evidence of attendance given at Parliament and councils* (Record Commission, 1827–34)
Parl. Papers	Parliamentary Papers
Parson and Parish	W.R. Ward (ed.), *Parson and Parish in Eighteenth Century Hampshire: Replies to Bishops' Visitations* (HRS 13, 1995)
PASE	*The Prosopography of Anglo-Saxon England*; www.pase.ac.uk
pers. comm.	personal communication
pers. obs.	personal observation
Pevsner, *North Hampshire*	M. Bullen, J. Crook, R. Hubbuck and N. Pevsner (eds), *The Buildings of England: Hampshire: Winchester and the North* (London, 2010)
Pipe R	Pipe Roll
PRS	Pipe Roll Society
Plac. de Quo Warr.	*Placita de Quo Warranto* (Record Commission, 1818)

Placit. in Domo Capit. Abbrev.	*Placitorum in Domo Capitulari Westmonasteriensi Asservatorum Abbreviatio* (Record Commission, 1811)
P.O. Dir. Hants.	*Post Office Directory of Hampshire, Wiltshire and Dorset* (London)
Poor Abstract, 1777, 1818	*Report from the Committee Appointed to Inspect and Consider the Returns Made by the Overseers of the Poor together with Abstracts of the said Returns* (Parl. Papers 1777 (157); 1818 4(02))
Poor Rate Rtns, 1825, 1830–1	*Select Committee on Poor Rate Returns: Reports* (Parl. Papers 1825 (334); 1830–1 (83))
Poor Rate Rtns, 1835, 1844	*Poor Law Commissioners: Third and Fourth Annual Reports* (Parl. Papers 1835 (444); 1844 (63))
Proc. Hants. F.C.	Proceedings of the Hampshire Field Club and Archaeological Society
r.	rod(s)
Rec. Com.	Record Commission
Reg. Cooper	HRO, 21M65/A1/27: register of John Watson and Thomas Cooper
Reg. Courtney	HRO, 21M65/A1/15: register of Peter Courtney
Reg. Fox	HRO, 21M65/A1/17–21: register of Richard Fox 1–5
Reg. Horne	HRO, 21M65/A1/26: register of Robert Horne
Reg. Pontoise	HRO, 21M65/A1/1: register of John Pontoise
Regs Sandale and Asserio	F.J. Baigent (ed.), *John de Sandale and Rigaud de Asserio AD 1316–25, Episcopal Registers: Diocese of Winchester* (HRSoc., 1897)
Reg. Stratford	R.M. Haines (ed.), *The Register of John de Stratford, Bishop of Winchester 1323–33*, 2 vols (SRS 42–3, 2010–11)
Reg. Waynflete	HRO, 21M65/A1/13–14: register of William Waynflete I–II
Reg. Woodlock	A.W. Goodman (ed.), *Registrum Henrici Woodlock, Diocesis Wintoniensis, A.D. 1305–1316*, 2 vols (Oxford, 1940–1)
Reg. Wykeham	T.F. Kirby (ed.), *Wykeham's Register*, 2 vols (HRSoc., 1896–9)
Rel. Census 1851	J.A. Vickers, *The Religious Census of 1851* (HRS 12, 1993)

Rtn of Parishes	Return of Civil Parishes in England and Wales under the Education Act (Parl. Papers 1871 (201))
Rot. Hund.	*Rotuli Hundredorum*, 2 vols (Rec. Com., 1812–18)
School Boards	Board of Education: List of School Boards and School Attendance Committees in England and Wales (Parl. Papers 1901 [Cd. 487])
Service, *Waverley Abbey*	M. Service, *The home estate, granges and smaller properties of Waverley Abbey* (Surrey Arch. Colls., 95, 2010) 211–57
SRS	Surrey Record Society
Stirling (ed.) *Diaries of Dummer*	A.M.W. Stirling (ed.), *The Diaries of Dummer, Dummer Reminiscences of an Old Sportsman, Stephen Terry of Dummer* (London, 1934)
Tax. Eccl.	*Taxatio Ecclesiastica Angliae et Walliae auctoritate Papae Nicholai IV*, *c.*1291 London, (Rec. Com., 1802)
TNA	The National Archives
unpubl.	unpublished
Valor Eccl.	*Valor Ecclesiasticus, temp. Henrici VIII*, 6 vols (Rec. Com., 1810–34)
VCH Hants.	*The Victoria County History of the Counties of England: Hampshire and the Isle of Wight*, 5 vols (original editions, London, 1900–12)
VCH Oxon	*The Victoria County History of the Counties of England: Oxfordshire*, 19 vols (London, 1902–2019)
VCH Surr.	*The Victoria County History of the Counties of England: Surrey*, 4 vols (London, 1902–12)
White's Dir.	W. White, *History, Gazetteer, and Directory of Hampshire and the Isle of Wight* (London)
Winton Dioc. Cal.	*Winchester Diocesan Calendar*
1939 Register	*1939 England and Wales Register, Hampshire, Basingstoke RD, EEDU*

The following technical terms may require explanation. Fuller information on local history topics is available in D. Hey, *The Oxford Companion to Local and Family History* (1996), or online at the VCH website (http://www.victoriacountyhistory.ac.uk). The most convenient glossary of architectural terms is *Pevsner's Architectural Glossary* (2010), also available for mobile devices.

Advowson: the right to nominate a candidate to the bishop for appointment as rector or vicar of a church. This right was a form of property which was often attached to a manor, but could be bought and sold.

Amercement: a fine imposed by a manorial court for an offence.

Commons: areas of land governed by agreements made at the manorial court, giving specified rights (e.g. of grazing a certain number of animals, or collecting furze) to certain people (e.g. the occupiers of ancient cottages).

Cottar: unfree peasant with fewer lands than villeins. Also called cottager.

Demesne: in the Middle Ages, land farmed directly by a lord of the manor, rather than granted to tenants. Although usually leased out from the later Middle Ages, demesne lands often remained distinct from the rest of a parish's land.

Enclosure: the process whereby open fields (q.v.) were divided into closes and redistributed among the various tenants and landholders. From the 18th century, enclosure was usually by an Act of Parliament obtained by the dominant landowners; earlier, it was more commonly done by private agreement, or by a powerful lord acting on his own initiative.

Glebe: land belonging to the church to support a priest.

Hagae: enclosures, usually with houses.

Hearth tax: tax levied twice a year between 1662 and 1688, assessed on the number of hearths or fireplaces in a house.

Heriot: a duty paid to a lord on the death of a tenant; originally a best horse or cow but later a financial charge (explained in panel on Manorial Courts).

Knight's fee: a medieval estate held for the obligation of providing an armed knight when required. Such obligations became increasingly theoretical or monetised, and by the 13th century many smaller estates were held as fractions of a knight's fee.

Manor: a piece of landed property with tenants regulated by a private (manor) court. Originally held by feudal tenure (see knight's fee), manors descended through a succession of heirs, but could also be given away or sold.

Messuage: a house with its surrounding land and outbuildings.

National School: a Church of England school affiliated to the National Schools Society for the Education of the Poor in the Principles of the Established Church.

Open (common) fields: communal agrarian organisation under which an individual's farmland was held in strips scattered amongst two or more large fields, intermingled with the strips of other tenants. Management of the fields, and usually common meadows and pasture, was regulated through the manor court or other communal assembly.

Probate inventory: a list and valuation of the moveable goods and livestock owned by a person when they died.

Tithe: a tax of one tenth of the produce of the land, which originally went to the church. It could be divided into great tithes (corn and hay), which went to the rector, and small tithes (livestock, wool and other crops), which supported a vicar.

Tithingman: the chief man of a group of ten householders, responsible for the group's behaviour, reporting infringements to the manorial court.

Tod: approximately 28 lbs of wool.

Turnpike: a road administered by a trust, which covered the cost of maintenance by charging tolls.

Villani: see Villein.

Villein: in the Middle Ages, a peasant tenant who technically belonged to the lord, suffered legal handicaps and usually owed labour services on the lord's demesne as well as rent. Villeinage gradually declined during the later Middle Ages. The earlier *villani* mentioned in Domesday Book enjoyed a freer status.

INDEX

Printed in the USA
CPSIA information can be obtained
at www.ICGtesting.com
JSHW070843070224
56802JS00009B/23